The Intelligent International Negotiator

The Intelligent International Negotiator

Eliane Karsaklian

First published in 2014 by
Business Expert Press, LLC
222 East 46th Street, New York, NY 10017
www.businessexpertpress.com

ISBN-13: 978-1-60649-806-4 (paperback)
ISBN-13: 978-1-60649-807-1 (e-book)

Business Expert Press International Business Collection

Collection ISSN: 1948-2752 (print)
Collection ISSN: 1948-2760 (electronic)

Cover and interior design by Exeter Premedia Services Private Ltd.,
Chennai, India

First edition: 2014

10 9 8 7 6 5 4 3 2 1

Printed in the United States of America.

Abstract

When reading this book you will be familiar with strategies, stories, facts, and tools that intelligent international negotiators use in order to succeed in their negotiations worldwide. The unique integrative cross-cultural approach to negotiating provided by this book will help you to have a different and innovative perception of what negotiating means today. Businesspeople negotiate every day, everywhere around the world. Some are more culturally aware and some are much less. Some forget that negotiation is, first of all, a human interaction. Some still think that negotiation rhymes with competition.

But after reading this book, you will approach negotiation from another perspective. More human, more pleasant, and more effective. The *Intelligent International Negotiator* is a ready-to-use book that you will read and digest very quickly, with inputs you will use immediately.

Enjoy!

Keywords

BATNA, cultural context, cultural dimensions, cultural intelligence, interculturalist, international negotiator's toolkit, myths, negotiation process, negotiation strategies, win-lose, win-win

Contents

Preface

Welcome to Your Personal Buffet

Negotiation and *international negotiation* traditionally have been presented as different activities in books and training sessions as if it were possible to separate them in the global markets we live in today. Some international negotiation books often provide useful country-by-country descriptions of how to negotiate with locals, without really explaining the reasons for such differences in behavior and the consequent impact on how business is conducted in each country.

Every Negotiation Is International

This book is different. I believe today's business negotiations are partly or totally international. Instead of artificially separating local from international negotiations, I use the cultural intelligence model to integrate them, presenting culture as part of—not separate from—the negotiation process. It is striking that negotiators still see culture as a side dish when it actually pervades and radiates meaning in every aspect of a company—and the whole field of business relationships (Trompenaars and Hampden-Turner, 2006).

Negotiation at every level includes concerns about decision making, establishing goals, designing strategies, interacting with people, and communicating in other languages—verbally and nonverbally. It's not my aim to make you understand each one of the existing cultures. Not only would that be unrealistic, it also could lead you to useless stereotyping.

Cultural norms are an *average*, and each individual is *unique*. Don't expect to get a list of dos and don'ts that tell you what is right and what is wrong to do in some cultures. If you stick to that kind of advice, what will you do when you meet people who behave totally differently from how they were *supposed* to behave? Your preparation would have been misleading and would create—rather than avoid—a gaff.

You Can't Be a Cultural Know-It-All

You may wonder, "How can negotiators know about all cultures?" They can't: It's not their job. There are the so-called interculturalists for that. The intelligent international negotiator masters *pertinent tools*, enabling him to work with all cultures. International negotiation is not about knowing *a* culture. It is about being able to work with *any* culture. Surprisingly, negotiators who know a specific culture very well tend to take it for granted, and they often do less preparation for their negotiation. This may lead them to take more risks than the person who doesn't know a culture so well.

Countless books and seminars have been created to teach negotiators about culture, as if their job was to understand and accept cultural differences. All over the world, there are training sessions conducted about how to adjust to diverse cultural environments. During these one- or two-day sessions, participants are told how to behave, live, and work in a culture. And the first thing the trainers say is that culture is complex and that we cannot learn about it in such a short time. So what's the point in attending these seminars?

Being an interculturalist is as much of a full-time job as being a negotiator. Negotiators take their lawyers, engineers, and financial experts to the negotiating table because they need their expertise. Think of interculturalists in the same way. Just as much you can't make an engineer or a lawyer out of a negotiator in a two-day seminar, you can't make an interculturalist out of a person with a simple training. We are talking about different and specific jobs.

Asia is a perfect example. Fortunes have been made by offering training sessions, conferences, and books to tell people about how to work with Asians. There are tons of publications about *working with the Chinese* alone. So you read all the books, take your dos and don'ts list, and fly to China to work with your local counterparts. How surprised will you be when you notice that they are totally Westernized because they've studied and worked abroad? Suddenly that cultural sensitivity list doesn't apply. You can't treat them as you were told because they don't really behave that way. You can't treat them as Westerners either because, after all, they are Chinese. So much for all of that time and money you spent on preparation!

As an intelligent international negotiator, you will know what to do. You take your toolkit to assess the people you will work with, and adapt the way you conduct your negotiation to that specific situation. It is much more realistic and efficient, because you will work with who they *are*, not who they were *supposed* to be.

Generalizations about cultures can be made, but you will always find exceptions. Think of your own country. Are all of your colleagues, clients, family, and friends the same? The aim of this book is to provide you with the awareness you need, the tools to understand the person you are working with, and which strategy would be the most effective. You will be well equipped to focus on your counterpart as a unique and specific person—rather than being trapped in stereotypes.

How to Digest This Book

This book is your self-service buffet. Everything is ready to be consumed. Help yourself and pick whatever you need when you need it. As a workbook, it's designed to be easily used in your negotiations, offering simplified theoretical concepts and ready-to-use tools. As there is no magic recipe for a successful negotiation, this book provides a variety of ideas, examples, and models. Pick those that suit your specific situation.

The ideas here draw on scientific research, combined with my decades of international field experience. To make this book as useful as possible for you, and make real-life negotiations come alive, I simplify the concepts, sum up the main information to master, and provide practical methods and tools.

The main goal is to help you become a better negotiator by providing a structured vision of the main aspects of your work. This will reduce uncertainty and complexity and help you better focus on what is really important in a negotiation. In addition, you will find many examples and critical incidents that I personally experienced. I hope you will relate to some of these situations and picture yourself experiencing each of the stories. That will keep this book about you rather than me.

The information is organized into four main chapters. At the end of each, you will find a box with one frequently asked question and the main takeaways.

Chapter 1 responds to common beliefs and myths about international negotiation. There is a lot of talk about how tough, stressful, or amusing international negotiation is. Now it's time to be realistic about it and understand this is neither rocket science nor an obscure, mysterious activity. It is negotiation that you practice by using the right tools and techniques in environments enriched by cultural differences.

Chapter 2 presents the main cultural dimensions and their impact on negotiation. You get insightful explanations about what leads to different behaviors across cultures. Understanding is the best way of not judging others and preventing stereotypes from getting in the way of your negotiations.

Chapter 3 provides an overview of the whole negotiation process. You will know how many dilemmas negotiators face, assess the role of trust and emotions in international negotiation, and be impressed by how much there is to be done during the preparation phase. This section includes everything you need to know about building relationships, bargaining, making decisions, and closing a negotiation. Negotiation styles, strategies, and tactics will hold no mystery for you anymore!

Chapter 4 will equip you with the ready-to-use International Negotiator's Toolkit (INT). By then, you will have started to master the tools presented throughout the book and will get an easy way to apply the cultural intelligence framework to your international negotiations.

Enjoy reading this book. Then get your suitcase ready to experience negotiating everywhere with everyone around the world!

Chapter FAQ

Do You Have Any Social Life at All?

As an international negotiator, you often travel around the world, which means your personal and professional lives need to be organized accordingly. This involves negotiating with your family and friends, who frequently misunderstand what you do and why you are always gone.

After a while, you realize that your best friends are the taxi drivers. They are the people you can talk to about the weather, family, tourism, politics, and, of course, traffic.

Your family and friends back home no longer wait for you to organize parties and related activities. Your social life is limited. But you now have worldwide friends. Wherever you go, you have people to visit and spend time with.

Thanks to this job, you meet new people every day. Will they become friends? Some might, some might not. But the truth is that there is no routine in your life, and that each day is an opportunity to learn, to discover, and to create new links.

CHAPTER 1

What International Negotiation Is Not

It seems *negotiation* has expanded from just a term we use in business. Now it's something that is integral in our daily lives.

Ask people, What's negotiation? Chances are you will hear words such as conflict, tension, winning and losing, concessions, price, and contract. Interestingly, this question will rarely evoke responses like dialogue, commitment, exchange, and culture. *Negotiation* has become a trivialized word that people use without knowing what it really means. That is why many people shy away from it, because they think that it implies conflict. When undertaken with confidence and understanding, negotiation is a creative interpersonal process in which two parties collaborate to reach superior results.

After all, why is negotiation important? There are only two ways of getting what we need in life: fighting or negotiating. Simply put, negotiating is a way for people to get what they need from someone else without physical aggression.

To be a successful international negotiator, you must feel psychologically comfortable in situations that involve uncertainty, unexpected behavior, measured risks, and decisions based on incomplete information. You need to think about resolving problems and creating opportunities with people who don't think and behave like you. That is why investing time in preparing your negotiations is so important.

This chapter will give you an overview of some common beliefs about negotiation and the counterarguments about them.

It Is Not All About Price

Ask people to do a negotiation role-play and they will focus on price—as if price were the only factor business negotiations were based on. This is a very narrow view of the field, and it prevents negotiators from seeing other solutions that form part of an agreement. More often than not, people get stuck in negotiations because the seller will not lower his or her price and the buyer will not accept the proposed price. However, there are many other aspects to be negotiated, such as delivery conditions, quantities, product customization, and such.

Here is one plausible explanation. Most business books, courses, and training sessions present negotiation techniques only based on price. One example is the main vocabulary they use: best alternative to a negotiated agreement (BATNA), reservation price, and zone of possible agreement (ZOPA).

BATNA states that negotiators will aim to get the best price for them: highest for the seller and lowest for the buyer. Both parties want to gain more than what they really need. BATNA is the standard against which a proposed agreement should be evaluated. It is the only standard that can protect a negotiator from accepting terms that are too unfavorable and from rejecting terms that are in his or her best interest to accept.

The reservation price is the lowest price the seller can propose and the highest that the buyer can accept without losing money (and the negotiation, of course). Finally, the ZOPA is a price range that would be negotiable between the two parties and lead them to a deal. Without ZOPA, there is no possible discussion, because it means the negotiators can't establish a common ground on price. It is also known as the *bargaining zone*. ZOPA refers to the region between parties' reservation prices. Its purpose is to determine if an agreement is feasible and whether or not it is worthwhile to negotiate.

This *quantitative* approach to negotiation hides the relevant *qualitative* side of it. Before anything else, negotiation is a human interaction. Companies do not negotiate: people negotiate on behalf of companies. Western negotiators are task-oriented and used to focusing on numbers instead of building relationships. But, as the world's economic power has shifted from North to South and from West to East, the theories about negotiation strategies and basics are to be adjusted.

You don't negotiate with the Chinese, Indians, Brazilians, and with any other more relationship oriented collective country the way you negotiate with North Americans, and Western and Northern Europeans.

These groups are more people- than contract-oriented. If all you can talk with them is about price, then you might miss making your deal. They have an iterative way of working, and they might be more flexible on price if you focus on more long-term aspects, such as commitment, privileges, and customized conditions.

To summarize, price does not generate loyalty, as the customer will always be attracted to anyone offering the lowest price. Other values lead people to compromise and create a longer term relationship. The negotiation process ends up being more subtle and time-consuming, but the outcomes are more sustainable—and less costly—in the long run.

Despite What You've Heard, Negotiation Is Not a New Trend

It has become fashionable to talk about negotiation these days. Business schools are creating courses on business negotiations. Professional trainers are developing negotiation sessions and coaching. The market has been flooded with books promising readers will win in all negotiations thanks to the techniques they would provide.

But neither negotiation nor international negotiation is new. The very first negotiators in the world—the Phoenicians in 1200 BCE—were naturally international. (Phoenicia was what we know today as Lebanon.) The Phoenicians were navigators, buying goods from one country and selling them to another. They knew where to find resources and what other parts of the world wanted them. Although their business world was limited to the Mediterranean coast, they traded goods internationally by providing their clients with products they would be unable to purchase in their own countries. As a pragmatic civilization, the Phoenicians stopped bartering and created the first currency in the world.

It Is Not Only a Matter of Win-Win or Win-Lose Strategies

Another common belief is that negotiation strategies are limited to win-win and win-lose outcomes. Either everybody wins, or someone must lose for the other party to win. Today's business ethics requires every negotiator to announce a desire for a win-win agreement. Win-win is considered good and noble, while win-lose is bad and should be avoided. No negotiator has the liberty of choosing a win-lose negotiation style: It is not politically correct.

So we negotiate in a world where everybody announces win-win intentions—without really understanding what that means. Indeed, what does *winning a negotiation* mean? How universal can this concept be? Is it about selling at the most expensive price, or buying at the lowest price? Or is it about collaborating with other people and getting what we need to do a better job? How vital can each negotiation be to all parties?

The answer might vary from culture to culture, which is why negotiating styles differ between countries. While the contract is the end of the negotiation process in some countries, signing an agreement is just the beginning of collaboration in others. In some countries, signing a contract is the goal, while in others the main goal is to create a network.

Some negotiators are skeptical about taking cultural differences into account. They say that business is business, and getting more by giving less is what counts. You may agree. But you should also remember that negotiators are people, and that people's minds are shaped by education, personality, and culture. Keep both in mind—business is business, but people are people. Doing this will help you understand that negotiating styles differ from country to country because people do not relate to others the same way. Thus, the old common beliefs about negotiation techniques and strategies might not apply to the new economic power-houses. There are emerging negotiating styles for emerging countries.

Negotiation is not a championship sport, where there is only one winner on a podium surrounded by two others who came close. It is about doing business. The goal is not being *better* than someone else, but *getting what you need* from someone else. If you start a negotiation with a competitive mentality—to beat the other side, ask yourself what you are going to do with those people once the negotiation is over. Unlike a sports contest, you don't say goodbye and go celebrate the triumph with your friends after the game is over. You get stuck working with them for a while—in an unpleasant relationship. And sure enough, next time you need to negotiate with them, they won't make your life easy. Negotiation is not a game.

But being nice is not the answer, either. You just need to understand that the people you are negotiating with are *not* your opponents. They are your counterparts, and you are negotiating with them because you need them. So it makes sense to be their partner, not their enemy. This way, instead of rejecting what they say, or openly disagreeing with them, take the process as it comes and reframe it in a more favorable way for you. This gives you the chance to talk about the issues from another perspective, which can be more productive for both parties. Reframing means taking what your counterpart says and directing it against the *issue*—not *him*.

It Is Not Only a Male-Dominated World

Most negotiators—international or local—are men. They were the first to get into this position in companies because they have been historically more independent to travel, compared with women who were needed at home to look after the family. Although this remains a male-dominated field, more women are getting involved. Having said that, it also is clear that more women are purchasers than sellers, probably because it is a more stationary position. Here's a good question: How many women have written books about international negotiation?

While the mentalities are evolving on women as negotiators, they are few in international settings. Often it does not seem natural to men to negotiate with businesswomen. It's also worth noting that women will never be able to negotiate in some countries, where business is exclusively a male activity.

While women might not appear as negotiators in several countries, often they are the ones pulling the strings from behind the scenes. Indeed, their role is to manage the budget and to make sure that the family's business goes well. They might not negotiate with strangers, but they will tell the men of the family how much they can spend and whom they can trust.

Consider the following situation. You are negotiating with a gentleman in India. You are both working in his office, and all of a sudden he invites you to go to a movie together. What do you do? I bet initially you are so surprised that you can hardly say anything! You have been invited for lunches, dinners, karaoke, and other more usual activities, but going to the movie? What for? We have work to do! You will feel even more surprised—and perhaps embarrassed—if you are a female negotiator.

Forget about your Western a priori and just accept the warm invitation. The man will certainly bring someone from his family to the movie, to get to know you in a more social setting. You will watch the film, have dinner, and—depending on how it goes—be deemed as trustworthy and secure the deal. There is one thing you can be sure about in such situations: no movie, no deal. By declining the invitation, you show you don't trust them. Then why would they trust you?

International Negotiation Is *Still* Negotiation

Successful international negotiators need to go beyond mastering strategies and tactics. They also must have a particular mindset: diligently preparing and planning, being creative, being flexible, and being curious about other people and cultures.

You may think the main difference between negotiation and international negotiation is the language. However, most international negotiations are conducted in English and, more often than not, negotiators don't work in their native languages. Some would even say that English has turned into something called *Globish*, which means Global English. It is a limited, usually conventional, vocabulary, supposed to be used and understood by all negotiators, independently of their mother tongues.

Even more important is the fact that language, in its broader definition, includes *nonverbal* communication. Negotiators need to hear what is *not* said. This aspect of intercultural interactions is much harder to understand than the array of English accents we may hear! To understand what has not been said, negotiators need to decode their counterpart's culture to avoid misleading interpretations.

Here is an important tip for negotiators from straight-talking countries. They should know that in several other countries, any type of open disagreement should be avoided. Instead, their counterparts will use indirect communication to express disagreement. International negotiators often get disappointed because they think that the negotiation went really well, but after a while, they realize that there is no follow-up from the other side. What sounded like an agreement to them was actually a negative response from the counterpart.

Stereotypes and Generalizations As Starting Points

The word *intercultural* often reminds us of stereotypes. Everybody has an idea about other cultures, and this often can be limited to a single characteristic. No negotiator is neutral vis-à-vis the counterpart's culture. Stereotypes are frequently deemed as being something bad. Well, they are not. Stereotypes are different from assumptions. They are part of a common, universal—however limited—knowledge of a culture. While rooted in history and tradition, stereotypes are a partial and superficial representation of it. The downside of stereotypes is when negotiators believe these give them enough information, so they don't spend the time and effort to dig deeper into the culture to get a broader view. In summary, stereotypes are just a starting point to get to know a culture, not a true representation of it.

Generalizations are created by assigning particular cultural orientations to a society or people. Be careful that these don't degenerate into stereotypes. Generalizations are initial hypotheses to be examined and modified through active engagement, while stereotypes are closed systems of belief. In other words, generalizations are a statement or an idea with a general and not specific applications. Stereotypes are a belief about people considered to typify or conform to one pattern, lacking any individuality.

Figure 1.1. depicts the cultural iceberg. It represents the main aspects of a culture. Invisible to others are the deep-rooted values, priorities, and assumptions—which actually are the underlying reasons for the visible customs, mores, and courtesies. By focusing only on what you see, you probably will judge people on their behavior without understanding it. To have a less stereotyped view of your counterparts, search for information about what you *cannot* see. The Cultural Analysis Grid (in your toolkit at the end of this book) will help you do that. Although it is impossible to know 100 percent about a culture (even your own), you should go beyond appearances to avoid being stuck in stereotypes.

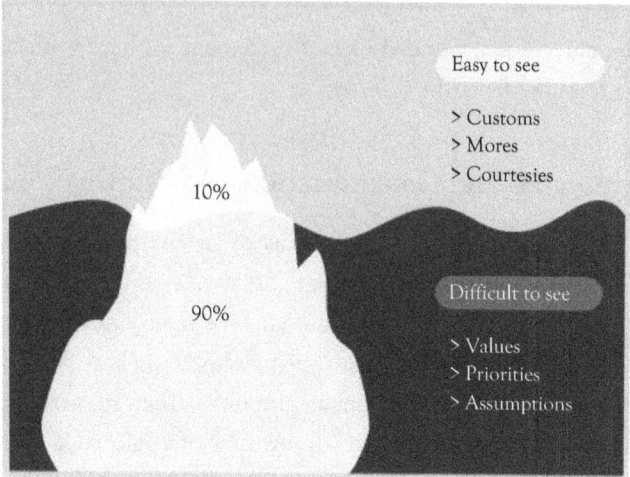

Figure 1.1 The cultural iceberg

The Seven Myths of International Negotiation: Total Cultural Homogeneity or Total Heterogeneity?

Sometimes people don't make the effort to understand cultural differences and their impact on business. Instead, they take comfortable shortcuts like the following:

- Myth 1: We're really all the same.
- Myth 2: I just need to be myself to really connect.
- Myth 3: I have to adopt the practices of the other culture in order to succeed.
- Myth 4: It's really all about personality.
- Myth 5: Business is business.
- Myth 6: Everybody wants win-win negotiations.
- Myth 7: It's about business, not about making friends.

The negotiator who believes those myths will be in trouble.

We can't be the same, because we don't have the same backgrounds. All people are shaped by national, cultural, and corporate environments, which makes it impossible to be the same. Being honest is the best thing you can do to be respected. However, being spontaneous is a big pitfall in international negotiations. The issue is that you tend to behave the same way you do back home, which may not be appropriate in the culture in which you're working.

In addition, avoid imitating others' behaviors. This might be seen as artificial—or even worse, as mockery. No one expects a stranger to behave as a local would. What people expect is some knowledge about and respect for the host culture. In any case, if you don't know how to behave in a given country, ask your counterparts what to do. Most often they will be pleased to explain their culture and help you by sharing some of their rituals. During any negotiation, asking for your counterparts' advice shows that you value them. You also will have more accurate information and take fewer risks than trying to figure out everything by yourself.

Cultures provide a source of identity for their members. In international business, we most often talk about country-based cultures. But cultures also develop around professions, organizations, religions, and so on.

How Can You Learn About Your Counterpart?

Let's move from cultures in general to the uniqueness of individuals and their personalities. The first bit of advice that negotiation trainers give you is to know about your counterpart's personality to better understand him and plan your counterattack. Now the question here would be, "How?" How do you get to know their personality? You can't expect them to take a personality test. In addition, you will be working with several people from the same country, and each one will have his or her own personality. How do you handle it? This advice does not sound realistic. But if you know the *culture*, you can have a better understanding of what guides their behavior in general.

The authors of the cultural intelligence model examined the relationship between the big five personality factors and the four-factor model of cultural intelligence (Ang et al. 2006). Their results demonstrated that a relationship existed that could predict behavior in international settings in terms of consciousness, agreeableness and emotional stability, extraversion, and openness to experience.

People who think that it is all about business, and that cultural differences do not matter, will be in big trouble. Although it is true that businesspeople do the same things all around the world, they do them differently. That happens because of cultural differences. And despite the politically correct discourse leading everyone to announce a win-win negotiation, that's not the aim of every negotiator.

Finally, in most cultures, making friends and doing business aren't considered separate activities. It is impossible to dissociate social and professional settings. If you are not part of the group, you are not in business with them. It might not always be about friendship as you define it. It has to do with getting to know the *person* they will work with, not just as a representative of the company. It has to do with empathy and trust. Being empathetic is focusing on the *feelings* of the other person, instead of their *actions*. People like to give things to people who listen to them, who value them, and who consult with them. That is why you need to know about people first.

Chapter FAQ

How Hard Is It to Be a Woman in International Negotiation?

First, you don't wake up every morning, look in the mirror, and say, "I am an international negotiator and a woman." You are just one more negotiator in the world. Although it is true that international negotiation is mostly a male-dominated field, being a woman has its plusses and minuses.

Sometimes your counterparts think it will be easier to negotiate with a woman. Many believe they can put more pressure on women and frighten them, or be less rigorous in their preparation because women are more intuitive, and similar stereotypes. If you are a woman, think of these as you would any other stereotypes people have about a culture. Then you'll have nothing to worry about: you play the game with them. But if you feel offended or threatened, your counterpart might take advantage. Surprise them by being professional and well prepared.

As a woman, don't be offended if you are not assigned to a specific negotiation. You know that some men refuse to work with women, and there are countries where you cannot be effective as a negotiator.

You might not agree with that discrimination, but your job is to do business with people and not to change their cultures. Leave that to diplomatic and institutional negotiators.

Chapter Key Points

- Think beyond price for other important terms to negotiate.
- There is a lot to learn with old school negotiators.
- There is more in international negotiation than winning or losing.
- Men most often are international negotiators, but they are more frequently selling to women as purchasers.
- The same techniques of negotiation apply to international negotiation—what changes is how they are used.
- There is no such thing as total cultural homogeneity or heterogeneity, because people are just people.

CHAPTER 2

Merging Culture With Negotiation

There is a lot of research about the influence of culture on business negotiations. However, while everybody knows that culture and cultural differences exist, not many have experienced it to know what they are really talking about. "Culture is like gravity: you do not experience it until you jump six feet into the air" (Trompenaars and Hampden-Turner 2006, 5). This chapter explores the main cultural dimensions, as defined by the most relevant researchers who specialize in cultural understanding. You will see how pervasive culture is in people's lives and its undeniable impact on negotiation.

What *Is* Culture?

There are more than 250 scientifically validated definitions of culture. The irony is that this can be explained by the lack of certainty about what culture really is. When analyzing human behavior, researchers were unable to use well-known concepts to explain some of it. That led them to say these factors are due to cultural specificities. No one really knows exactly what culture includes and, as stated by Tylor (1913), "culture is a complex whole that includes arts, morals, laws and any other capabilities acquired by men to be a member of a society."

While there are many definitions of culture, they all share two common aspects: culture is a group-level phenomenon, and it is learned. Values, beliefs, and expectations about behavior are passed from one generation to the next. This creates general guidelines for the acceptable manners of conduct within a society.

Culture has an impact on social or professional behavior because it shapes people's mentality and dictates norms that all members of the society follow. Culture is rooted in deep values: both conscious and unconscious. Ask yourself if you would be able to explain to some foreigner why you do things the way you do in your country. You are more likely to answer, "because this is the way we have been doing it forever" than to explain the real reasons. Since culture is specific to one society, this implies cultural differences among different societies. That leads us to the cultural differences we face in our day-to-day international business relationships.

The Impact of Culture on Negotiation

Culture has three obvious impacts on negotiations. First, there is the mindset. Depending on how people were alphabetized, they will be more verbal or more visual. Second, there are the norms that dictate behaviors. For example, the way we should address people, taboo topics we are not allowed to bring up, the food we eat and the way we eat it, and so on.

Third, negotiations require a great deal of social activity. These integrate rituals and traditions important to locals. As an international negotiator, you are supposed to know about them and be open to participate in some of them. As an example, when negotiating in some Middle Eastern countries, you might be surprised to be invited to weddings and other family parties, especially if you don't have a close personal relationship with your counterparts. The objectives are twofold: first, they need to take you out of the office to get to know you better as an individual. They would also want to see how flexible and open-minded you are. Second, they organize huge parties for such celebrations. The more people who attend them, the better. It's a sign of power.

International etiquette has long been used as a key factor in books and training sessions about international relationships. You are informed about how to greet people in different countries, which topics to avoid, gift-giving practices, and business card exchanges. Although this is relevant and useful, it is not enough when you're preparing for a negotiation.

Observing cultural social norms is paramount to understanding human behavior. But a negotiator should know about the impact of culture on negotiation strategies and styles. Culture influences negotiation on several levels: individual or team negotiation, the amount of time needed to reach an agreement, the value of concessions, the amount of social life integrated in the negotiation process, the influence of family, and risk taking, just to name a few.

Although a little understanding is better than nothing, it might not be enough to enable people to negotiate internationally. Studying and understanding other cultures is a different job. Negotiators might make a lot of effort to get to know other cultures, but they can never specialize in it. The best alternative is to be accompanied by someone who *can* specialize. Negotiators then may focus on their strategies and leave the cultural understanding to an expert who can open the doors for them.

Research suggests that people negotiate differently when they are with people from their own culture versus those from other cultures. *Because cultures develop to facilitate social integration, it follows that social integration will be lower when there are multiple cultures in a group (Stahl et al. 2009).*

Overcoming the "My Culture Is Best" Bias

Triandis (2006) adds the inescapable reality that all humans are ethnocentric. That is, they strongly believe that what is normal in their culture should be normal everywhere. Anything different is abnormal and wrong. To overcome this bias requires a great deal of effort because, to some extent, it goes against human nature. If you only know one cultural system, it is inevitable that you will be ethnocentric. Overcoming this requires an ability to put yourself in someone else's shoes. But this can entail a tendency to question one's own cultural norms, which can make people feel uncomfortable. That is why international negotiators must have considerable adaptability.

Now that we are talking about tolerance, acceptance, and nondiscrimination, it seems like everybody is open-minded and ready to adjust. We might think that it is natural to accept cultural differences—but it's not. People are self-centered and don't want to make a lot of effort to understand differences or to adjust. Negotiators leave it to the balance of power: the one who needs the other party more badly has to adjust. Some cultures are easier to adjust to than others. It depends on the cultural distance.

Understanding Cultural Distance

Cultural distance is the gap between your culture and other cultures. The bigger the gap, the bigger the distance and, thus, the bigger the effort needed to adjust. It also requires more effort to find common ground between the parties, since they don't share similar values and behaviors.

Consider the following situation. You accompany a French client on a one-week negotiation in Chicago. You think that it will be easy, because France and the United States are developed Western countries and so the cultural distance might not be significant. Throughout the week, however, you realize that you are having some trouble getting your French client to work productively with the Americans. They don't manage time the same way. They use agendas differently, and their mindsets are definitely different.

However, everything goes well until the closing gala dinner. The day before, your French client is invited to sit at the table of honor. He is flattered and looks forward to the event. The next evening, by the end of the predinner drinks, he tells you that he expects someone to accompany him to the table. You explain him that he is expected to go to the table at the scheduled time, as he has accepted the invitation. After a while, when everyone already is seated, he joins you at your table. He complains that Americans don't know how to look after their guests. On the other hand, the Americans at the table confirm their stereotypes about the French being unreliable, because they do something different from what they say.

Cultural "Animals"

One way of finding similarities among cultures is by comparing them to animals, which was done by Lewis (2012). Some cultures are like cats, some are like dogs, and others are like horses.

Cats tend to dominate others. They are independent, loosely loyal, and know how to charm others when they need them.

Dogs are happy to be dominated as long as they get something in return, which can be physical (such as food) or psychological (like love). They are extremely loyal and reliable.

Finally, horses are bigger than humans but agree to be dominated. They are hard workers, but there are some rules that should not be broken (mounting from the left side, for example) or the consequences can be dangerous. A horse obeys coded signals sent by the horseman with the reigns, but can bite him or throw him off if it is not happy with the treatment it receives.

Maybe you realize that your culture (or just you) is more like a dog, a cat, or a horse. And you know that cats and dogs don't get along well, but it is not impossible to bring them together. Dogs have little respect for cats. Cats think that dogs are weak, without any personality. Horses can tolerate both dogs and cats, but know they will never do anything together, because of their considerable difference in size and speed.

It is easier to represent human personalities by using metaphors such as animals. Cartoons are a good example. People feel freer to laugh at or to criticize them, which is not nearly as acceptable to do with other human beings.

Another useful aspect of analyzing animals when trying to understand intercultural relationships is to see that they don't mix species. They live in tribes and defend their survival and territory. Most importantly, they preserve their race. By extension, tolerance and acceptance of other cultures is not natural to humans either. We must learn to be open to other races, cultures, and rituals. That is why it requires a great deal of effort and willingness to work with other cultures.

Culture Through the Eyes of a Child

It you want to know what behavior is natural for human beings, observe children. They are spontaneous before they socialize. They like novelty but not differences. They reject other children who are not like them, and often with some cruelty. After being socialized, they learn not to behave this way and that they must accept differences. As adults, this is what negotiators do when working with other cultures: accepting that differences exist and trying to cope with them in order to work together.

We also receive an inconsistent education throughout our lives. As children, we reject and accept only what is useful to us. We claim what we need anytime we need it. We follow no social rules. As soon as we start socializing in kindergarten (or even at home), we learn to separate and classify objects by colors and shapes. When a child wants to put a triangle in a place designed for a square, he is corrected because his choice is wrong. Special toys are created to prevent children from inserting anything that isn't the right shape.

The same thing is true with colors. When children mix objects with different colors, they are corrected and told to group the blues with the blues, the greens with the greens, and so forth. Then, when we are adults, we are told to accept people with different colors, shapes, and mentalities.

The Importance of Respect

Cultural differences in negotiators' behaviors imply that the environment for the negotiation might not be naturally favorable. Not respecting cultural etiquette might not doom your negotiations, but it will make it harder to get what you need from other people. Your counterparts will have more respect for you if they see that you have studied their culture and have some knowledge about it. In addition, you will feel better prepared and less vulnerable if you know more about the other side's culture.

Intercultural interactions in negotiation are not about adjustment, they are about respect. You are not expected to become one of them. You are expected to behave consistently with your culture as well as to be culturally aware to respect local norms. As such, you are not expected to wear the local clothes, but to respect the local dress code by wearing your own clothes. Your counterparts already have a certain perception or knowledge of your culture. Stereotyped or not, it is the way they see your culture and expect you to behave accordingly.

People know more about some cultures than others. They expect certain behaviors from you. For instance, the American culture is broadcast worldwide thanks to movies and TV shows. Although these might not represent all Americans, they give an idea of the country's way of life to other cultures. In contrast, some other countries—such as Armenia or Paraguay—are obscure to more than half of the world's population, because information about them rarely is shared. That is why negotiators must also have some country-specific information.

The Myth of a "Global Culture"

The dilution of cultural differences into a more global culture is more a myth than reality. Cultural specificities are getting even stronger in some emerging cultures, which wish to maintain their independence from historically dominating cultures. This means negotiators need to think like cultural translators. They should be able to decode both words and behaviors, as some cultures might use proverbs and metaphors to say "no" or to convey any disagreement.

When working with African counterparts, you might hear such quotes as, "To run is not necessarily to arrive." "However long the night, the dawn will break." The first proverb will tell you not to rush people. In African cultures, people take their time to live, to get to know other people, and to build relationships. You will get nowhere with them if you try to rush. You will be perceived as a cold, distant person, unable to enjoy interacting with others.

The second proverb shows you their fatalistic mentality. What is to happen will happen sooner or later. The way may be tough, but it will eventually happen, and there is not much you can do about it. You cannot take hasty initiatives or try to control the situation and the events, because this is not the way they understand and handle life.

"Saving Face" and Disagreements

Finally, negotiators need to know how to disagree or to explain themselves without making others look bad. You have heard about the importance of saving face in China, and this concept is true elsewhere. People in several other countries are concerned about preserving their and others' faces and want to avoid unpleasant and conflicting situations.

It is easier to understand this when you know that losing face is about dignity, sense of honor, and consistency. It is *not* just about disagreeing with someone else in front of others. If you are not aware of the cultural norms, there is a high probability that you will be rude without even knowing it.

Once a Brazilian purchaser was waiting for a reply from a Japanese supplier about a certain product. After several weeks with no news from the supplier, despite her reminders, the Brazilian purchaser started pursuing him by phone and e-mail. When he did not reply, she lost her temper and sent a very assertive message. She asked him directly if he really wanted to work with her company—with several question marks at the end of her sentence. If so, she suggested that he do his job properly. Even worse, she copied his and her own supervisor on the e-mail.

She did not realize how much damage her action would cause to the Japanese counterpart. If she had been culturally aware, she would have asked him about peripheral topics, which would then lead him to answer her main question. She would know that he would never give her a negative answer or make her aware of any problems he was having with her request.

The Role of Communication

You understand that communication plays a crucial role in negotiation. Worldwide, nonverbal communication accounts for about 65 percent of how people get information. In many cultures, behavior counts for more than half of the message being conveyed. You must know about implicit communication to understand what your counterparts are telling you, without saying it with words. If you are unable to observe and decode their behavior, you will miss very important information.

Do not expect people to say everything clearly. Some cultures have a greater behavioral component in their communication, while others are just implicit and say different things with the same words. There is also what is called second degree communication. In this case, the interpretation depends on the pronunciation and the emphasis on specific words. You are supposed to read between the lines. Typically, these are cultures where people don't take you at your word and always look for something behind them, "What did he mean by that?"

Consider the following situation. You are working with a Brazilian counterpart on a project, and you are ready to sign the deal. The few times you have interacted with him, he said that everything was OK on his side. When you finally meet to sign the agreement, the Brazilian avoids talking about your business topic, keeps smiling and making jokes, and creating brief diversions.

After playing his game for a while, you get to the point and ask him about the agreement. You realize his company has done nothing. But he would never have told you because that would involve losing face, and he was probably waiting for the solution to appear by itself or from someone else. Ideally, he would be expecting that you had not done *your* job, either. You certainly surprised him by having everything completed on time.

The All-Inclusive Verbal and Nonverbal Communication

If you get confused and ask your counterparts to be more explicit about what they mean, that won't improve matters. From their perspective, they already are being clear. Moreover, they are not always conscious of which portion of their communication is implicit versus explicit. To them, it is just communication. Actually, what *you say* is less relevant than what *they hear*. Make sure that there is consistency between both sides. What sounds confusing to you may sound loud and clear to others.

Putting Cultures in Context

Hall (1976) identified two extremes of a cultural dimension, depending on the cultural context. After having analyzed 11 cultures, he placed them in a continuum, stretching from high-context to low-context cultures.

He defined *low-context cultures* as the ones in which the communication is more objective: with a small portion of nonverbal messages and less dependent on relationship building. In these cultures, social and professional lives are clearly separated. On the other end of the continuum, he placed *high-context cultures*, which are more implicit. They add a considerable amount of nonverbal communication and include personal relationship and the practice of rituals as part of their professional relationships.

In other words, low-context cultural environments expect and reinforce making meaning explicit. They block out the potential interference of nonverbal or other contextual sources. In high-context cultures, the successful exchange of information hinges on the ability to apply a shared and implicit framework of interpretation to a message. Some of

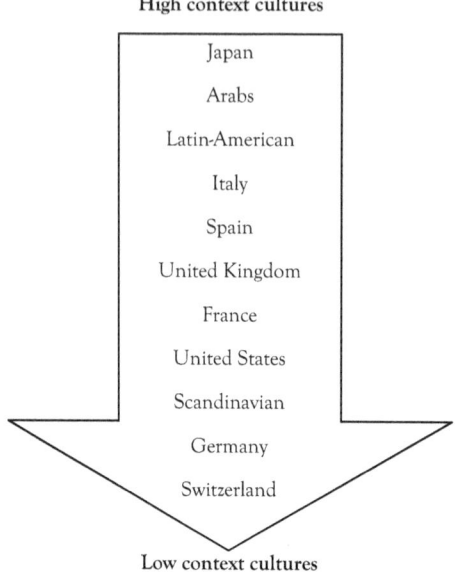

High context cultures

Japan

Arabs

Latin-American

Italy

Spain

United Kingdom

France

United States

Scandinavian

Germany

Switzerland

Low context cultures

Figure 2.1 From high- to low-cultural contexts

the cultures he analyzed, ranked from higher to lower context, are represented in Figure 2.1.

In some cases, Hall analyzed one country. In others, he grouped countries into regions. Make sure that when you work with a specific country in one of those regions, you understand the cultural differences among them. For example, if you work with a Latin American country, you need to know that they all belong to a high-context culture, but they have their own specific culture.

Another important aspect to take into account when using Hall's model is to understand the relative value of it. For example, negotiators from the United Kingdom are perceived as implicit and difficult to assess by the Germans, but too direct and assertive by the Arabs. Countries such as France, the United Kingdom, Italy, and Spain (which are in the center the model) are more complex to understand, and people's behaviors are hard to predict. They can be seen as being very objective or very subjective, depending upon who is doing the comparison.

Once a French purchaser was working with a Swiss counterpart. When he had a technical problem with a machine produced in Switzerland, he called his counterpart to ask him for some help, because they have a good relationship. After greeting his Swiss counterpart the French negotiator asked him if he knows how to fix the machine. The Swiss answered, "No." The Frenchman was upset. He expected that his counterpart would automatically help him to find someone else to fix the machine. He did not realize that the low-context Swiss had just answered to the question he had asked. If he wanted further information, the Frenchman would need to ask more questions.

It is worth noting that of the 38 cultures analyzed by Hall, only 12 are low context. That means you are more likely to work with high-context cultures in international negotiations.

Cultural Relativity

Everything about culture is relative. The concepts and the models created by researchers are often represented by continuums in which we can locate countries by comparing them with others. In doing so, we tend to say that Country A is more objective than Country B, which is more particularistic than Country C, which in turn is more individualistic than Country D.

Think about the trips you have taken. You will remember every place that attracted your attention by the strangeness or uniqueness of local people doing something differently from your habits. It is through comparison that you get to better know your culture of origin and the new one you are in.

Everything seems normal in the country where you were born and raised, because people tend to follow the same norms, which is why you take your culture for granted. The first time you go abroad, you are surprised to notice different ways of doing the same things. Intrigued by that, you compare and try to understand where the differences come from and which alternative best fits you.

This comparative approach is called *cultural relativity*. Everything is relative, and absolute measures do not make any sense in international settings. The most salient expression of cultural relativity is time management. You may spend the same amount of time on two different activities. One of them will seem to be time well invested, and the other one a waste.

Your counterpart from other culture may have exactly the opposite perception. For example, negotiators from low-context cultures perceive small talk and conversations about private lives a waste of time. On the other hand, negotiators from high-context cultures gladly invest time in their negotiation by getting to better know the person they are likely to work with.

Would You Rather Have Peaches or Coconuts?

Another very important aspect in building a relationship with counterparts is to know about how and what people like to communicate with each other. Some people are like peaches: soft, agreeable to touch, sweet, and easy to get along with. These people talk to strangers, are easy going, readily speak about their private lives, and make other feel comfortable—as though they were already friends. But when you want to go deeper into what looks like friendship, you bump into the pit. They do not wish to reach a deeper level of intimacy with you. Anglos, Latin Americans, and Africans are some examples of peaches.

Then there are the coconuts. They are hard to get into. You need adequate tools to break the hard shell. But once you are in, it is sweet and agreeable and there are no more obstacles. Negotiators from Europe, the Middle East, and Asia are examples of coconut cultures. The metaphor was coined by the German-American psychologist Kurt Lewin in the 1920s, when he was working with Americans (peaches) and Germans (coconuts) and studied the reasons why they find it difficult to understand each other and work together.

Language Barriers and Translators

Cultural differences can greatly interfere with the communication process. Effective communication requires people to have at least a minimum of shared language around which to align. Different country-based cultures often have different languages. Even when they share a common language, they may not always translate meaning in the same way. The different values and norms among people from different cultures make it difficult for them to find a shared platform or a common approach (Stahl et al. 2009).

If you think that everybody can speak English, you are just partially right. More companies from non-English-speaking countries are adopting English as their working language. It does not mean, however, that all their negotiators feel comfortable when negotiating in English. And even when the negotiations take place in English, there are always those moments when the other team will speak in their native language, which you cannot understand, and you will wonder what is going on. In addition to getting familiar with many different accents in English, you should also be ready to feel (or look) comfortable when the other party interacts frequently in its mother tongue, even though you do not understand it.

Without trying to speak *all* needed languages, you should at least know some basic words in order to show interest and respect. It will be greatly appreciated if you can greet and thank people in their own language. However, you should avoid using terms and expressions that are restricted to the locals, because you do not follow their implicit meaning. One example would be those that relate to religion.

Just as no negotiator can speak all needed languages, no one can know about all cultures. These are different jobs. Being a negotiator is *not* being a translator, nor is it being an interculturalist. Negotiators have the choice between (1) negotiating in English and being aware of the limited understanding they will have with non-native English speakers, or (2) asking for an interpreter, whose job is to translate.

Likewise, negotiators can attempt to know about cultures themselves. They may try to negotiate well in all cultural contexts while having limited understanding of them, or they can be accompanied by a person whose job is to deeply understand all cultures. Even if you can speak other languages, you have a hard time trying to translate sentences into your own language. This happens because translation and interpretation have specific techniques that it takes people several years to learn.

The same happens with interculturalists. You may know about some cultures and be able to use some tools to keep moving ahead with your international negotiations, which is the goal of this book. But you will never be able to perform as well as when you are accompanied by a person who masters all the tools and has been prepared to interact with other cultures for years.

All cultures don't have the same relationship with their language. This means that some are pickier about the excellence in mastering their language. They want to avoid having you *massacre* it by turning to English as soon as you start speaking their language. Others will feel flattered and will be happy to help you with pronunciation and vocabulary.

For example, the French are very picky about their language. They can hardly bear someone who can't speak French properly, and they would rather switch to English or any other language they can speak instead of listening to someone who speaks French poorly. Consistently, French negotiators are known for having few language skills and for feeling uncomfortable when negotiating in English. This is because the French in general don't allow themselves to speak a language that they can't master at the same level as their mother tongue—so they don't practice it.

A common way of overcoming language barriers in negotiation is using translators. They have the big advantage of saving you the effort of speaking other languages and preventing misunderstandings due to word choices. Translators also can help people to save face. In a recent visit to Japan, the president of France called his audience *Chinese*. The French-speaking attendees were shocked, but the translators saved him by replacing his word with *Japanese*.

But using interpreters might sound easier than it really is. First, you will need to find an interpreter with some technical knowledge, to talk about your offer with the same accuracy that you would. Second, you cannot be sure about what and how your message is being interpreted. Because you cannot understand what the translator is telling your counterpart, you can only hope that the other party is getting the message you really want to convey. Because of that, negotiators often take their own interpreters to the negotiating table just as they do with their own lawyers. Then one interpreter can supervise the other one to make sure that there is no misinterpretation.

This is a real concern for negotiators, because having other people stand between you and your counterpart will slow down negotiation. You will not be in charge of timing and able to give the needed emphasis to what you want to say. Interpretation of nonverbal communication might be disturbed as well. You may be surprised to see that what was supposed to be *your* negotiation ends up being *the interpreters'* negotiation, because they spend so much time supervising and correcting each other.

Finally, intercultural communication is about encoding and decoding. All languages are codes we use to communicate with each other. These can be gestures, words, and facial expressions. Communicating with people from other cultures is not much different than communicating with cats, dogs, or horses. As they don't understand your words, you need other cues to help them understand what you say. Pavlov demonstrated that phenomenon by classical conditioning, when he taught his dog to understand a ringing bell meant that its food was served.

The Pitfalls of Distant Communication: Videoconferences, Conference Calls, E-mails, and Other Technology-Based Communication

Financial turmoil has caused companies to search for ways to reduce costs, including cutting travel expenses. As a result, negotiators are turning into distant negotiators. They discuss price, delivery, and other relevant topics via conference calls and videoconferences. Using technology-based communication is a clear advantage in business, as it offers the benefits of speed and being in touch with counterparts as often as needed at very low cost. The disadvantage is that a considerable amount of nonverbal communication is hidden, and building a relationship is almost impossible. There is nothing that you can experience together with your counterpart by using Skype, MSN, or any other real-time communication technique.

But e-mails don't prevent negotiators from socializing. You can always add some off topic or personal interactions with your counterpart. You also can be friendly and enthusiastic. However, it is much harder to interpret emotional undertones in e-mail communications. Finally, it prevents the projection and identification phenomena between people facing each other, which is so important to create empathy.

Using e-mail is undoubtedly very comfortable. But remember the message you write today is colored by the feelings you have today. The person who receives your message will not read it in the same mood you were in when you wrote it, and should be able to understand the message you are trying to convey. Sometimes when you are in a time crunch, you just reply to an e-mail very quickly. Understand that this can be taken as rudeness on the other side.

The use of smartphones is also very convenient, as it makes negotiators accessible all the time. The tricky aspect is that you might be
tempted to reply immediately—without giving much thought to the
subject—and use inappropriate language. In addition, the short length
and abbreviations used in texting—sometimes exacerbated by the phone's
autocorrect function—greatly increases the likelihood of unintended
misunderstandings.

Moreover, the use of smartphones is not practiced or accepted in the
same way everywhere. In some cultures, people will check their messages
and take calls during a meeting, while in others this is perceived as very
disrespectful. Research demonstrated that people using their smartphones
during a negotiation are perceived as cheating, because they are getting
more information than the other side. You can use this situation to create
a concession in a negotiation that is underway. By using his phone while
you did not use yours, you may say that your counterpart has unbalanced
the negotiation terms, so he (implicitly) owes you a concession to get the
negotiation back in balance.

Conference calls are used every day by international negotiators.
These can be very confusing when there are several people talking at the
same time—on one or both sides. Indeed, if there are a number of people on the call, you might be confused during the discussion and not
know exactly who is saying what. This phenomenon is compounded if
you work with polychronic cultures, in which people handle several tasks
at the same time.

Polychronic Versus Monochronic Approaches to Tasks

Polychronic individuals go back and forth on the same activity, paus-
ing when they are interrupted by other tasks or other people. They don't
mind stopping something in favor of something else, and then coming
back to what they were doing before. Also, they feel comfortable when
someone cuts them off during conversations and do not get lost when
many people talk simultaneously.

If you are a monochronic person—who handles one task at a time—
you might feel a bit lost in this environment. These people schedule and

allocate specific time slots for each activity. They lose their place when they are interrupted and get very disturbed when several people talk at once. Moreover, in monochronic cultures, meetings start and finish on time. The agenda is followed from top to bottom, and once a topic was already discussed, it is not revisited.

Here is another aspect to take into account. If you insist on reaching an agreement separately for each issue in your agenda, it might not only *not* suit your polychronic counterparts, but also prevent you both from having a more holistic view of the whole deal and finding better possibilities for trade-offs.

On the other hand, the polychronic negotiators feel comfortable in situations where several activities are happening at the same time. They view time as more flexible and spend a good amount of it just talking with people about superficial and informal topics. The agenda is not sacrosanct, and even when the meeting is over, they might remain to interact with others. Being late or postponing appointments is usual in polychronic cultures.

These differences in time management are meaningful. Assign a monochronic and a polychronic person with the same three tasks. After a while, the polychronic will be able to tell you a bit of each one and how she is handling them, but she will probably be late to hand them in and might negotiate the deadline.

At the same time, the monochronic will be just able to tell you about the first task, because he would not have started any others before he is done with that one. He will be able to go deeper into the description of what he has been doing for the first task, but unable to tell you about the remaining ones. This might be misleading, as you might think that the monochronic has not understood that there were three tasks to be done. However, he will respect the deadline and finish the three projects on time.

Main Cultural Orientations

Hofstede and Hofstede (2005) state that the world is full of confrontations between people, groups, and nations who think, feel, and act differently. At the same time, these people are exposed to common problems that demand cooperation for their solution.

Culture is defined as a mental programming, because all people carry within themselves patterns of thinking, feeling, and potential acting that were learned throughout their lifetimes. Much of this information was acquired in early childhood, because that is when a person is most susceptible to learning and assimilating. As soon as certain patterns have established themselves within people's minds, they must unlearn these before being able to learn something different—and unlearning is more difficult than learning for the first time (Hofstede and Hofstede 2005).

The authors also point out that culture should be distinguished from human nature and personality. Human nature is what all people have in common. Culture is always a collective phenomenon, because it is at least partly shared with those who live or lived within the same social environment. Culture is learned, not innate. It comes from one's social environment, not from one's genes. Personality is one's unique set of mental programs that need not be shared with any other human being. It is based on traits that are partly inherited from the individual's unique set of genes, and partly learned, as shown in Figure 2.2.

In analyzing cultural differences, Geert Hofstede identified four major dimensions of culture and mapped their distribution among managers from more than 70 countries, as seen in Table 2.1.

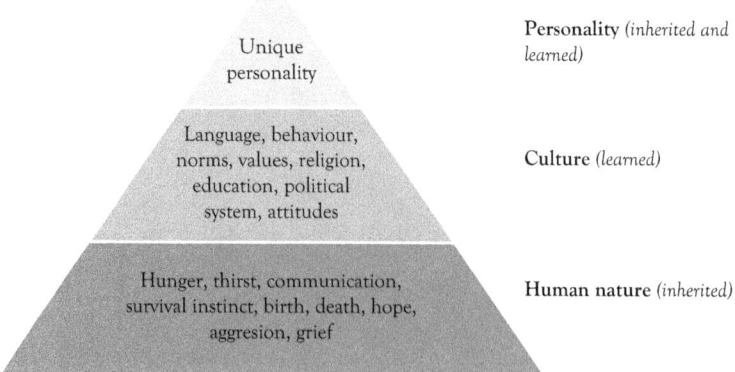

Figure 2.2 Hofstede's pyramid of human uniqueness

Table 2.1 Hofstede's cultural dimensions

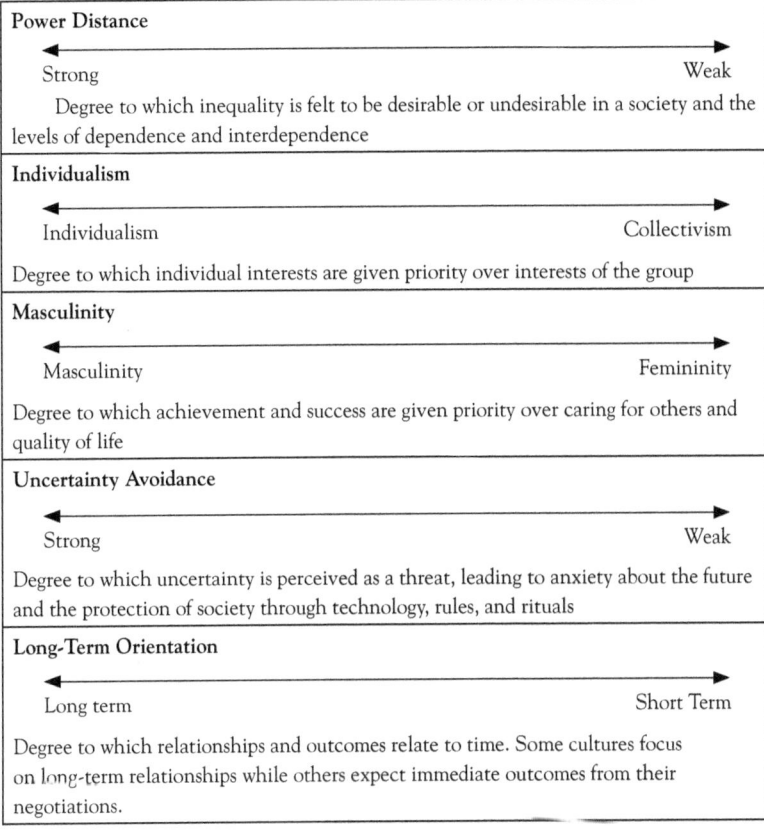

Power Distance
Strong   Weak
Degree to which inequality is felt to be desirable or undesirable in a society and the levels of dependence and interdependence
Individualism
Individualism   Collectivism
Degree to which individual interests are given priority over interests of the group
Masculinity
Masculinity   Femininity
Degree to which achievement and success are given priority over caring for others and quality of life
Uncertainty Avoidance
Strong   Weak
Degree to which uncertainty is perceived as a threat, leading to anxiety about the future and the protection of society through technology, rules, and rituals
Long-Term Orientation
Long term   Short Term
Degree to which relationships and outcomes relate to time. Some cultures focus on long-term relationships while others expect immediate outcomes from their negotiations.

According to Hofstede and Hofstede (2005), national cultures will affect negotiations in several ways:

- *Power distance* will affect the degree that control and decision making are centralized, and the importance of the negotiators' status.
- *Collectivism* will affect the need for stable relationships between negotiators. In a collectivist culture, replacing a person means that a new relationship must be built, which takes time. Mediators have an important role in maintaining a viable pattern of relationships that allows progress.
- *Masculinity* will affect the need for ego-boosting behavior and the sympathy for the strong on the part of negotiators and their superiors, as well as the tendency to resolve conflicts by

a show of force. Feminine cultures are more likely to resolve conflicts by compromise and to strive for consensus.

- *Uncertainty avoidance* will affect the (in)tolerance of ambiguity and (dis)trust in opponents who show unfamiliar behaviors, as well as the need for structure and ritual in the negotiation procedures.
- *Time orientation* is the fifth dimension the authors identified. It relates to short- and long-term results and relationships.

To understand the impact of Hofstede's cultural dimensions on negotiation, consider the graph in Figure 2.3.

The American negotiator belongs to a flatter and more individualistic culture, so is more autonomous in decision making and will probably negotiate alone. His Chinese counterpart will be part of a team of negotiators and will need hierarchical approval of any decisions. Although there is not much difference in terms of masculinity, the Chinese might be more concerned about the negotiation failing than the American, who, by the way, will be also less inclined to take risks than the Chinese—who have a lower score for the uncertainty avoidance dimension.

There is a huge gap between both cultures in time orientation. The American negotiator will focus on short-term results and would rather go faster with the negotiation process without spending (wasting) much time in building relationships. However, his Chinese counterparts will spend as much time as needed before getting to a deal. They focus on long-term relationships. They need to invest time in getting to know the

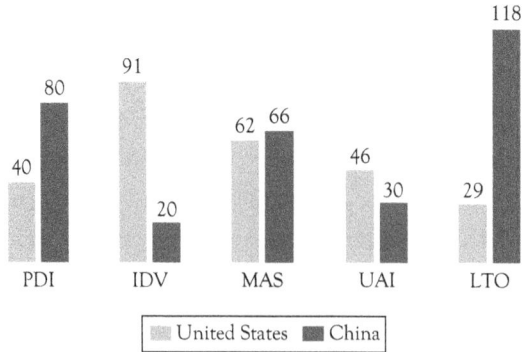

Figure 2.3 Cultural differences between the United States and China
Source: www.geert-hofstede.com

people they will be working with. Finally, the American negotiator will focus more on signing a contract as a way of closing the deal. His Chinese counterparts will look for a long-term relationship through collaborative work once the contract is signed.

Everybody seems to be puzzled by the rapid deployment of Chinese investments around the world. Analyzing the scores presented previously can easily explain this. As people belonging to a strong hierarchical culture (power distance), the Chinese obey and honor the elderly. This means both parents and government are investing in the younger generations, so this group may make their contribution to take China to the top of the most powerful economies in the world. To do so, the Chinese go abroad to study, to work, and to run companies. Nothing—from new languages to new disciplines—seems to be a barrier to their determination to achieve their goals (masculinity).

The country's low score in uncertainty avoidance explains how much of a risk the Chinese are willing to take. However, they take risks collectively, which is reassuring to them. They are always in groups with other Chinese, and they stick together wherever they are (collectivism). This allows them to speak Chinese and eat familiar food, benefitting from Chinatowns spread throughout the main cities in the world. Their long-term relationships explain why they only work with people from their families or with other Chinese. It is a matter of trust (long-term orientation).

Trompenaars and Hampden-Turner (2006) explain cultural differences as each culture choosing specific solutions to certain problems that reveal themselves as dilemmas. Thus working in international settings is about reconciling the dilemmas, as shown in Table 2.2.

Affective negotiators are warm and welcoming. They show their feelings (genuine or not) when they are happy or unhappy with how things are going with the negotiation. Neutral negotiators feel uncomfortable with these expressions, as it looks fake and un-businesslike to them. They would say, "Why should we be delighted? We're just doing our job here." Russians, for example, find it hard to trust someone who uses gestures, moves around, and shows facial expressions when speaking. They think that their interlocutor is creating a diversion from the substance of a negotiation and might be untrustworthy.

Those who are self-oriented will take responsibility for the negotiation. This person will feel more concerned about the outcomes of the

Table 2.2 Reconciling dilemmas in Trompenaars and Hampden-Turner's cultural dimensions

Affectivity Feeling, emotion, and gratification	**Affective neutrality** Practical or moral considerations
Self-orientation Self-interest	**Communitarianism** Group goals and interests
Universalism Using common standards to evaluate situations and groups	**Particularism** Using different standards to evaluate situations and groups
Ascription Stressing who you are	**Achievement** Stressing what you do or have done
Specificity Interaction for specific purposes	**Diffuseness** Interaction across a wide range of activities

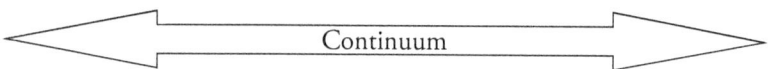

Continuum

negotiation—and the job she is doing—rather than how the rest of the group performs. In universalistic cultures, negotiators have a binary view of life: things are divided between what we are allowed to do and what we are not allowed to do. All people are submitted to the same rules.

By contrast, in particularistic cultures, norms are obscure and depend on the person. What is *not* possible to someone *is* possible to someone else. There is a lot of favoritism in particularistic cultures. Your negotiations will go nowhere if you are not friends with the *right* people. More companies are trying to avoid the bribes developed by these cultures, in which being friends also means doing favors. Gift-giving practices are being coordinated, and negotiators are just allowed to offer their company's goodies to stop with the flow of luxury products being used as persuasion tactics in negotiations.

If you belong to an achievement-oriented culture, you might be more interested in your counterparts' achievements as a businessperson and a negotiator than in his personal background. But if your counterpart is from an ascription culture, she is more likely to investigate your private life to identify your family name and the networks you belong to. She might also be more interested in your diplomas than in your working experience.

Finally, negotiators belonging to a diffuse culture mix private and professional lives. In Japan, for example, the boss is also a father, and should protect his employees. As a result, the employees are at the boss's and the company's disposal at any day and time. There is no way that they will leave the office at 5:00 p.m. as people do in other countries.

If you are a negotiator from a specific culture, you will work from 9 to 5 and then leave time for your private activities. What happens when you become an international negotiator and go to Japan, a diffuse culture? Your counterparts will pick you up at any time (day or night) and at any day of the week you arrive. They will take you to your hotel, make sure that everything is arranged, and then take you to visit and dine with them. They will look after you and take you everywhere throughout your sojourn in Japan because, in a diffuse culture, accompanying you at all times is part of doing business with you.

Businesspeople from diffuse cultures are always disappointed when they negotiate in specific cultures, because they don't receive the same treatment. More often than not, they have a map, directions to the meeting place, and the time for the meeting. They are taken to a dinner and a lunch, and the rest of the time they are on their own.

Values and Communication

Lewis (2012) states that human beings organize their lives around two core features: values and communication. These elements usually remain constant in a person's behavioral make-up. This is principally true because people—when faced with the trials and vicissitudes of life—have a strong urge to seek security in traditional behavioral refuges.

Lewis' LMR model divides cultures into three categories:

- *Linear-active people* tend to be task-oriented, highly organized planners who complete action chains by doing one thing at a time, preferably in accordance with a linear agenda. Speech is for information and depends largely on facts and figures.
- *Multiactive people* are loquacious, emotional, and impulsive. They attach great importance to family, meetings, relationships, compassion, and human warmth. They like to do many

things at the same time and are poor followers of agendas. Speech is for opinions.

- *Reactive people* are good listeners and rarely initiate action or discussion. They prefer first to hear and establish the other's position, and then react to it and formulate their own opinion. Reactives listen before they leap. Speech is for creating harmony.

Now you know why negotiation is above all a human interaction, and this is the reason why culture has such an impact on it. If negotiators from different cultures behave differently, it is because their cultures are anchored on different values. Lewis described anchors for the three types of cultural categories, as demonstrated in Table 2.3.

The anchors described in this table represent what is valued in each type of culture—and by its negotiators. If you are a negotiator from a linear culture, you need tangible elements—such as products, facts and figures, and contracts—to get to a deal. However, a multiactive negotiator will search for personal commonalities, persuasion based on emotions, and tell about things instead of proving them with concrete measures. Finally, the reactive negotiator never disagrees, does not demonstrate emotions, and uses the network as a guarantee for a deal.

Cultural anchorage influences decision-making preferences across cultures, as represented in Table 2.4.

It is paramount to know about cultural values in negotiation, because you need to create value before you claim it when you are bargaining. Getting to a deal implies that all counterparts are happy with the out-

Table 2.3 Cultural anchors according to Lewis

Culture	Characteristics	Anchors
Multiactive	Talkative, warm, relationship-oriented	Family, hierarchy, relationships, emotions, eloquence, persuasion, loyalty
Linear-active	Scheduled, factual, task-oriented	Facts, planning, products, timelines, word-deed correlation, institutions, law
Reactive	Listening, accommodating	Intuition, courtesy, network, common obligations, collective harmony, face

Table 2.4 Cultural preferences according to Lewis

Type of culture	Preferences
Linear-active	Compromise Take a vote (majority rule) Debate vigorously and come to some conclusion Use common sense Let's decide today Let implementation follow quickly Avoid ambiguity Dislike chopping and changing Decisions are final
Multiactive	No piecemeal decisions Let's discuss everything comprehensively Lateral relations must be considered Majority rule has a fundamental weakness: the minority might be right Matters need not all be decided today Bosses make decisions: have we consulted them? There is no such thing as international common sense A good decision is better than a consensus or compromise Relationships are more important than a hard-and-fast decision
Reactive	There is nothing new under the sun Decisions, therefore, should be based on best past precedents Decisions are best if they are unanimous One should not submit to the tyranny of the majority, but reason with all until unanimity is achieved A harmonious decision is better than an acrimonious one, however convincing

comes of the negotiation, and the condition for it to happen is that all parties get what they value.

Schwartz and Bisky (1987) studied the motivational goals underlying cultural values and identified 10 fundamental values. Schwartz's works represent the most comprehensive exploration of cultural values to date. His typology, presented as follows, has been found to be universal and stable across gender, age, socioeconomic groups, cultures, and generations.

- Achievement (personal success through demonstrating competence according to social standards)
- Hedonism (pleasure and sensuous gratification)
- Stimulation (excitement, novelty, and challenge in life)
- Self-direction (independent thought and action; choosing, creating, and exploring)

- Universalism (understanding, appreciation, tolerance, caring about humanity and nature)
- Benevolence (preserving and enhancing the welfare of loved ones, friends, and family)
- Conformity (restraint of actions and inclinations)
- Tradition (respect, commitment, and acceptance of the customs and ideas that traditional culture or religion provide the self)
- Security (safety and harmony, and the stability of society, relationships and self)
- Power (social status and prestige, control or dominance over people and resources)

Schwartz also empirically demonstrated that if you place these values in a mathematical two-dimensional space, they will form the so-called circumplex structure: the values with similar motivational goals will end up closer to each other, and the values with conflicting motivational goals will be further apart, as shown in Figure 2.4.

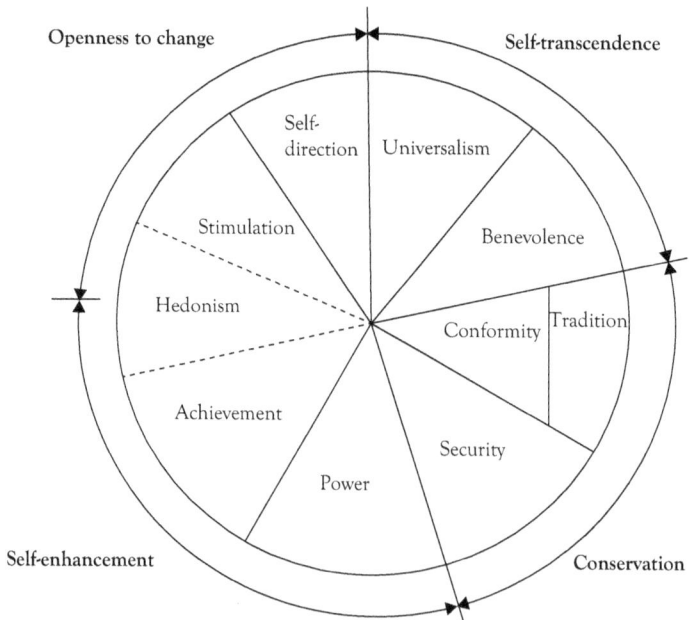

Figure 2.4 Schwartz's fundamental values

When analyzing this graph, you can imagine how a negotiation between people from opposite sides would look. Those on the conservation side would be more reluctant to take risks and less open to innovation. They would stick to what they know and would not be defined by creativity. This means the open-to-change negotiator needs to be reassuring and slowly introduce new ideas or alternatives to the deal. In addition, the self-enhancement negotiators would want to achieve the best deal for themselves, because they like power and need to show what they are able to accomplish. However, they will have a hard time trying to persuade the self-transcendent negotiator, who is more altruistic and looks for universal benefits.

To understand the roots of cultural differences in avoiding or competing in conflicts, you need to understand cultural values. Self-enhancement and achievement. Conformity and tradition. The traditions view to negotiations—associated with the Western world—would be to deal rationally, focus on economic capital, have dispositional attribution, and use direct information and direct voice. In contrast, the alternative view to negotiations—applicable to many non-Western countries and regions—would use emotionality in making concessions, focus on building relationships and social capital, demonstrate situational attribution, and use indirect information sharing and indirectness in communication (Khakhar and Rammal 2013).

More recently, Global Leadership and Organizational Behavior Effectiveness (GLOBE) was conceived by Robert J. House (House et al. 2004) of the Wharton School of the University of Pennsylvania in 1991. It involved 170 country co-investigators, based in 62 of the world's cultures, as well as a 14-member group of coordinators and research associates. To aid in the interpretation of findings, the researchers grouped the 62 societies into 10 societal clusters or simply clusters, as shown in Figure 2.5.

In the GLOBE model, it is useful to know which clusters you and your counterparts are in. Then you should refer to the other researchers' dimensions to know what characterizes the cultures you will be working with. If you are in the Anglo cluster, you know that it will be easier for you to find commonalities with other countries from the same cluster. You share several cultural traits, such as being linear-active, and having

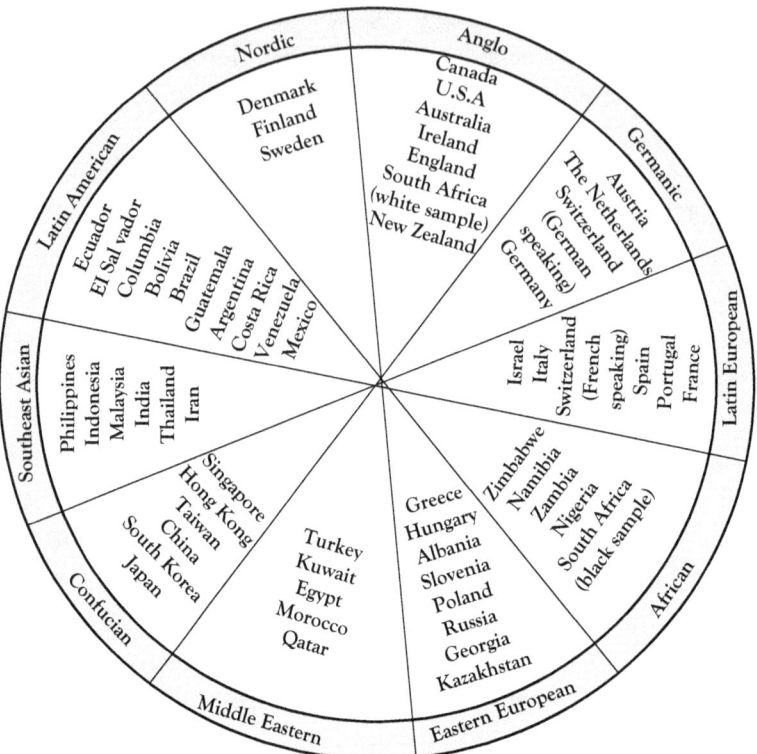

Figure 2.5 The GLOBE 10 societal clusters

low scores in power distance and in uncertainty avoidance, and high scores in individualism and masculinity. You will also tend to be more universalistic, achievement-oriented, and specific.

Consider the following situation. A French manager was looking for partners in India. He hired a specialist in international business to help him. The international expert made several trips to India to identify the appropriate potential partners and to open the doors for the French manager. Each time the international expert was back in France reporting to him, the manager was unhappy because he believed nothing tangible was coming from so many trips to India. He would say, "We are spending a lot of money with your trips to India, and you always come back empty-handed." Once the international expert had everything sorted out for the French manager's first visit, he decided to go to

India alone. He told the specialist, "You've been there several times and came back with nothing. I don't need you there with me. I know how to handle it."

Indians belong to a diffuse culture. This means they were at the airport waiting for their French guest when he landed. However, the French manager had already booked a limousine to take him to his hotel, which he had insisted upon using, rejecting the one suggested by his potential Indian counterparts. After the Indian hosts had waited long enough in the airport to understand that their guest had gone to the hotel by himself, they called him at his hotel to say they would pick him up for dinner. He replied, "If you want to have dinner with me, it should be in my hotel's restaurant." Needless to say, the Indians never arrived.

What happened? The hasty and arrogant approach of the Latin European is totally inconsistent with the humble and face-saving, long-term oriented Southeastern Asian values. What was carefully built across months by the international expert was destroyed in a couple of hours by the culturally unaware manager. What did he learn from the experience? Nothing. He believed that the international expert was incompetent and wasted a lot of money traveling to India, and that Indians are rude because they did not come to see him at his hotel when he had traveled to their country just to meet them.

The 10 Cultural Orientations Model

Walker and colleagues (Walker et al. 2003) define culture *as* a complex phenomenon that can be determined by three axioms:

- *Axiom 1*: Cultural boundaries are not national boundaries. Although it is easier to describe nations as cultures, and generalize behaviors, there are cultural commonalities across countries, and there are subcultures in each country.
- *Axiom 2*: Culture is a shared pattern of ideas, emotions, and behaviors. Cultures operate both in a conscious and unconscious level, and their characteristics are carried by groups and individuals.

- *Axiom 3*: Cultures reflect distinctive value orientations at various levels. The specificity of culture is that it lies in the difference between in and out groups. People who share the same culture sense that they are different from people who do not belong to that culture.

These authors created the 10 Cultural Orientations Model, which presents a framework of exploring and mapping components of culture at any level. It is the cornerstone of the cultural orientations approach and provides a common language and comprehensive lens for analyzing cultural phenomena and cross-cultural encounters. This set of cultural dimensions summarizes the main aspects that can explain cultural differences and cause misunderstandings in business settings. They are described in Table 2.5.

These cultural orientations permeate individuals' professional and private lives. Knowing about them will help you to not only understand why people you will be negotiating with behave as they do, but also to anticipate some of their behaviors. Let's analyze each of them.

Environment

Environment indicates a person's basic relationship to the world at large. Negotiators who like to control the environment are more likely to rely

Table 2.5 The 10 cultural orientations

Cultural orientations	Characteristics
Environment	Control/harmony/constraint
Time	Monochronic/polychronic, fixed/fluid, past/present/future
Action	Being/doing
Communication	High/low context, direct/indirect, formal/informal
Space	Private/public
Power	Hierarchy/equality
Individualism	Individualism/collectivism, universalism/particularism
Competitiveness	Competitive/cooperative
Structure	Order/flexibility
Thinking	Deductive/inductive, linear/systemic

on schedules and to avoid any surprises and improvisations. Anything that was not planned is very disturbing to them. Those looking for harmony with the environment will pretty much integrate it into their negotiations. They will try to control some aspects of it, such as time and weather, but are conscious of the fact that not everything is foreseeable. Finally, negotiators who see the environment as a constraint will let things happen and cope with them as long as they happen. To them, things just happen when they must, and there is nothing people can do other than conform to it.

Perhaps you have experienced the following situation. You are working with your Egyptian counterparts in their office in Cairo. Around 5:00 p.m., they tell you that it is time to leave because you are invited to a dinner at home of their company's president. Your reaction might be, "Why didn't you tell me about this before? I am not prepared!" Of course, if you say that, you will make your counterparts lose face. Instead, you go to the dinner wearing your work clothes and without knowing how much business you will talk about over the dinner.

This is the way things can happen in cultures where the environment dictates people's lives. They are so used to taking life as it comes that they don't even think about planning things in advance. Of course, they knew about the dinner long before your arrival in Egypt. But they wouldn't let you know about it, because they would be going with you, and also because the dinner could have been cancelled at the last minute for any reason. So they just wait and see, and behave accordingly. The lesson is be prepared to never be prepared. You should always imagine that something you didn't anticipate could happen, whatever it is. Just make sure you are ready to talk or not talk about business at unexpected moments with unexpected people.

Time

The use and views of time convey messages about what is valued in a given culture and how people relate to each other. We already described monochronic and polychronic people and how they manage time and tasks. Consistently, monochronic negotiators are punctual and scheduled. Time is fixed to them and being late looks un-businesslike. In addition, monochronic negotiators have a linear conception of time, and the past, present, and future do not mix.

In contrast, polychronic negotiators take their time to socialize and to conduct simultaneous activities. Time is fluid, and the definition of punctuality is subjective. Past, present, and future are not clearly dissociated, and negotiators may lose today to win tomorrow, because opportunities come and go across time.

If you work with Brazilians, you will experience authentic polychronic situations. First, all participants won't be at the meeting at the same time. Brazilians make several appointments at the same time and juggle them. They take phone calls during the meetings and constantly go in and out of the room. If you are monochronic, you are more likely to feel lost and upset with these situations, since you believe every meeting has a starting and an ending time to be respected. You follow your agenda and have things done quickly, with all the people around the negotiation table at the same time.

Although it is sometimes overwhelming, you should plan more time when you work with polychronic people. Avoid making several meetings with different people the same day, as you never know what time your appointments will start and end. Moreover, your meetings may well end up moving to a restaurant, a bar, or another less formal setting. Once a delegation from the Netherlands in Brazil stood up at the time when the meeting was supposed to be over and rushed to their next meeting. However, for the Brazilians, the meeting was just starting. As a result, their negotiation with the Brazilians ended that very moment.

Action

Action focuses on the view of actions and interactions with people and ideas that tend to be expected, reinforced, and rewarded in a given culture. Negotiators belonging to a *being* culture value people's personal and professional backgrounds. It is more important to *be* someone than to have accomplished important things in life. This means senior negotiators are more respected, the family and network are highly valued, and relationship is the bedrock of negotiation. It relates to what Trompenaars called ascription cultures.

On the opposite side of this dimension are achievement-oriented cultures. What you have accomplished as a professional counts much more than who you are. These cultures value experience more than diplomas and rely on facts and figures. Also, they respect confident negotiators with extensive field experience.

Take your résumé and show it to a negotiator from a doing (action-oriented) culture and to one from a being culture. They will focus on different aspects of your background. The doing-oriented negotiator will look at your jobs and accomplishments, versus the being-oriented negotiator, who will focus on your family name, your degrees, and your network. The first one will respect you because of your achievements; the second one values your personal traits.

Communication

There are different formats for expression and exchanging information. You have already seen the high and low communication context countries. High-context negotiators focus more on building relationship than on contracts and invest time in getting to know their counterparts personally. They stay away from direct communication, and part of their messages is indirect and nonverbal. These negotiators avoid conflicting situations and losing face. But the way they address you can be either formal—as with the Japanese—or informal—as with the Latin Americans.

Low-context negotiators are more time-oriented, get straight to the point, don't need to get to know their counterparts personally to negotiate with them, and base their trust on contracts. They practice direct communication and can be either formal—like the Swiss—or informal—like Americans.

Another aspect of communication was introduced by Trompenaars through the neutral and affective dimension. Neutral negotiators are inexpressive and don't use gestures or facial expressions to convey their messages. On the other hand, affective negotiators use emotions to convey either positive or negative messages. So neutral negotiators perceive affective counterparts as people who exaggerate, making a whole drama out of a simple argument. However, affective negotiators perceive neutrals as inhuman, cold, and inexpressive people. It is annoying to them to be unable to read their counterparts' expressions to see whether or not they agree with what is being said.

Talk to the Chinese and you will have no clue of what they think about what you just said. They will not nod, they will not smile, and they will barely look at you. Ask them a question, and you will get no answer. Ask them if they understood what you said, and they will answer "yes." You might feel very uncomfortable with their moments of silence, which will feel as if they last forever.

Then you fall into the traditional pitfall. You think that they didn't understand what you said, and you rephrase, you add more information, and you give a more detailed explanation. Or worse, you think that they disagree and won't say so openly. Then you hastily come up with other ideas or concessions as if they had make objections—which they haven't. Silence and facial inexpressiveness are part of Chinese communication. There is nothing that you can do about it except to wait until they break the silence and continue the conversation. Silence is communication, so don't interrupt it.

Space

Cultures can be categorized by the distinctions they make in their use and demarcation of space. If you belong to a culture where the space bubble is small, then you feel comfortable with physical closeness. Negotiators from these cultures tend to greet people with hugs, look for eye contact, and stand and sit close to each other. But if you belong to a culture where your bubble is bigger, then you might feel as if your privacy was invaded when others are too close.

The difficult aspect of this in negotiation is that in cultures where private and public spaces are mixed, people often feel rejected by those who step back when they greet them or talk to them. Scenes where one negotiator steps forward to talk and the other steps back at the same time might look hilarious to outsiders, but they are serious business to the one who feels rejected and the other who feels invaded.

E. Hall is the cultural anthropologist who coined the term *proxemics* in 1963 (Hall 1963). He emphasized the impact of proxemic behavior (the use of space) on interpersonal communication. Hall believed that the value in studying proxemics comes from its use in evaluating not only the way people interact with others in daily life, but also the organization of space in their houses and buildings and, ultimately, the layout of their towns.

In cultures where physical closeness is appreciated, people might want to talk in places where you can sit side-by-side instead of the opposite sides of a desk or of a meeting room table. It might make negotiators feel more comfortable about delivering precious information. He defined three types of bubbles of space, as represented in Figure 2.6.

Consider the following situation. You are queuing up somewhere in Cairo. Since your bubble of space is bigger than theirs, you keep some distance from the person in front of you. The Egyptian behind you asks you to step forward. You perceive this as getting too close to the person ahead of you without making the line move any faster. But if you don't do that, some other people will take that tiny space and move you farther back in the line. You will not only feel physically uncomfortable but also upset with the rude Egyptians, who are unable to respect order of arrival and cheat openly before your eyes.

This example illustrates the business mentality of cultures where the bubble is small: all vacant places are to be taken before someone else does. When negotiating with them, make sure that you are not leaving any unfilled spaces both in your relationships and in your arguments, where someone else could sneak in.

Power

Hierarchy-oriented cultures value social stratification and accept differing degrees of power, status, and authority. Hierarchy has a clear impact on negotiators' behaviors. The stronger the hierarchy, the weaker the

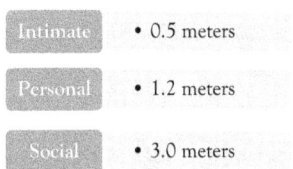

Intimate	• 0.5 meters
Personal	• 1.2 meters
Social	• 3.0 meters

Figure 2.6 Personal bubbles of space as defined by Hall

negotiators' autonomy to make decisions. Hofstede stated that hierarchy was a matter of power distance. In strong power distance cultures, there are several levels of management and negotiators are not allowed to report to upper levels, but only to their supervisors. They need approval for their actions as well as for concessions they can make during a negotiation. As a result, strong power distance tends to slow down negotiations, because negotiators' ability to make decisions is restricted.

The consequences are easy to understand. If you are from a weak power distance culture, you may not be patient enough to wait until your counterparts get replies and approvals to keep going with the negotiation. As a more autonomous negotiator, you are able to make decisions by yourself and assume the consequences for these. You may even see their relationship with their manager as childish and may lose part of your motivation (or patience) to work with them.

A French manager hired an American negotiator to develop the company's business with North America. The American negotiator believed he would work with the same level of responsibility and autonomy that he had in the United States. After 6 months, the American had developed no business at all. The French manager said that the American had no motivation. The American said that he never had a clear definition of his objectives as a negotiator, quit, and went back home.

What happened? The French manager never shared the whole project with the American negotiator. He supervised every action the negotiator took, more often than not telling the American that this was not the way he should work. The negotiator was lost, with no goals and autonomy, and wondered what his role was in such a company.

Individualism

Cultures differ in the way they value and perceive identity based on affiliation versus individual achievement. Both Hofstede and Trompenaars presented a cultural dimension measuring the degree of belongingness of an individual to a group.

In individualistic cultures, negotiators are more independent. They negotiate by themselves or in teams with a limited number of members. On the other side, collective negotiators create teams with several members, and each is assigned a specific role by the team leader. It is their obligation to measure the impact of the outcomes of their negotiation on the rest of their group. They have a clear idea of how much the group depends on them and how much they depend on their group. As an Australian negotiator once said after his first round with Koreans, "Next time, I will bring more people on our side too."

It is worth noting that often the word *individualism* is confused with *selfishness*. That is far from truth. Individualistic countries are more communitarian, that is, individuals look after themselves but respect the rules to make sure they are not disturbing other individuals' lives.

Collectivistic cultures tend to award privileges to and protect only their close groups. They don't care about those whom they don't know—even if they are part of the same community. You will also notice that people from individualistic cultures are more generous. They take more charitable actions and have the sense of giving back to the community, while in collectivistic cultures, people share what they have with the groups close to them.

Trompenaars adds the universalistic and particularistic cultural dimension. He stated that universalistic cultures are more egalitarian than particularistic cultures, because they apply the same rules to everybody. So universalistic negotiators will observe the company's rules no matter whom they are negotiating with, while particularistic negotiators are more inclined to make exceptions depending on the person they are working with.

Rules are clearly stated, understood, and observed in universalistic cultures, while they are obscure in particularistic cultures, where favoritisms are frequent. If you are a universalistic negotiator, you constantly have the feeling that you missed something, such as a relevant bit of information. All of a sudden—and with no apparent reason—concessions that were impossible to do before turn out to be possible now, or vice versa. As there is a very strong attachment to the individual in particularistic cultures, negotiations are highly dependent on personal relationships between the counterparts. You need to become friends with them to get what you want.

An English negotiator went to Colombia. Although he could speak good Spanish, and his counterparts were fluent in English, the negotiation couldn't work out—because he needed to stick to his company's rules and make no exceptions. In addition, he could not understand the favors the Colombians were asking him for through indirect communication, because they were not clearly saying it. They used common expressions, such as "Now that we are friends, we can think differently. We are doing everything for you to feel comfortable among us." His patterns of universality prevented him from being more customized in his negotiation. That led his Colombian counterparts to perceive him as too rigid.

Competitiveness

Competitiveness addresses deep drivers of action, choices, decision, and customs. Negotiators are always confronted with the cooperation or competitiveness dilemmas of their counterparts, as if they were obliged to choose one of them. It also relates to win-win (cooperative) and win-lose (competitive) negotiation strategies. Some cultures are more competitive because being excellent is the norm and competition is defined by being better today than yesterday.

Hofstede defines cultures as being masculine and feminine. Masculinity values competition, materialism, and professional achievement. Femininity draws on values such as harmony, cooperation, and general well-being. So competitive negotiators are more contract- and efficiency-oriented, while cooperative negotiators are more concerned about saving face and building long-term relationships.

Let's say you are from a masculine country (and thus competitive) and you will be working with Swedish counterparts, who are very feminine. You would want to know that at the outset. Initially, you will feel comfortable because you might share some cultural dimensions, such as individualism, flat hierarchy, short-term orientation, universalism, and punctuality. This might lead you to negotiate with them in the same competitive way you would with a company back home. You will head right into a problem. The Swedish are extremely feminine, and harmony and equality are key characteristics of their culture. They will put their cards on table, wishing to build a winning situation for all—not only for the negotiating parties, but for everyone who could be directly or indirectly affected.

Structure

Structure recognizes different perspectives and attitudes toward change, risk, ambiguity, and uncertainty. Order has to do with being scheduled and rigid with time and tasks. Negotiators need to know about their schedules, meetings, topics to be treated, people participating in each meeting, and so forth. They wish to plan—as a way of avoiding uncertainty—and feel uncomfortable if plans change. They perceive this as a lack of professionalism and organization.

Negotiators from flexible structures are much less concerned about schedules, time management, and order. These people might take things as they come and are not disturbed by surprises because they are good at improvisation. They feel uncomfortable with a counterpart's rigidity, perceiving him as a person who isn't creative enough to cope with unplanned situations.

Assume that your Lebanese counterparts come to work with you in your home country. You've been working with two of them all afternoon and invite them to have dinner at 7:00 p.m. around 5:00 p.m., one of them tells you that he has another meeting and should leave. You are a bit disturbed but ask him if he will still join you for dinner. He says that he would be most happy to do so and asks you for the address to get to the restaurant. Once he has left, you want to keep going with the negotiation with your other counterpart. Then you realize no progress is being made because he is not the decision maker. Then you end up taking him to visit some of your building facilities and head to the restaurant for dinner.

At the restaurant, you order some drinks and tell the waiter that a third person will join you shortly, and that you will wait for him to order. Meanwhile, you keep socializing with your counterpart. At 7:50, you still don't know where the other negotiator is—or even if he is coming to the restaurant. Your other counterpart seems fine about it.

Around 8:30, the other negotiator calls you to tell you that he will be there very shortly. After 30 minutes, he arrives and brings along the other person he has been working with until then. You end up having dinner with three other people, unable to talk about your business because of the unknown person at the table (who, by the way, you will never see again) and paying the bill for four people instead of three. As a result, you will need more time the next day to continue negotiating with them. This is how the people in unstructured cultures behave. Everything is possible, and flexibility is important to them. What you would have considered as being rude is just normal to them.

Thinking

Thinking concerns a culture's propensities for conceptualization. Deductive thinking leads negotiators to see the big picture first to understand what they are talking about, and then get down into the details. Priority is given to the conceptual world and symbolic thinking rather than to facts.

Inductive thinking negotiators take the opposite approach. Models and hypotheses are based on empirical observation and experimentation, and the goal is verification through empirical proof. Different thinking patterns may lead negotiators from both styles to the same outcomes, but the process is very different. This opposition creates misunderstandings because they don't see the same issues at the same time. They frequently say, "I don't understand where you are going with this."

It also has to do with systemic or linear thinking. The systemic negotiator makes associations among all the information gathered and considers the impact of each decision and concession on the whole business. Linear negotiators chunk the negotiation into parts, and each part seems to be independent of the others. In doing so, they will treat each point separately, while the systemic negotiator will have a more holistic approach. Some negotiators begin with agreement on general principles and proceed to specific items (top-down approach) while others begin with agreement on specifics, the sum of which becomes the contract (bottom-up approach).

Observe how Americans and the French do presentations. The American will introduce the topic, give the big picture, get into some details about the main points, and wrap up by presenting the key takeaways, telling people where they may find all the remaining details, and then take questions.

The Frenchman will give an outline of his presentation, which will be structured in chapters, subchapters, headings, and subheadings. After a long introduction, he will explain—in detail—each point in each chapter. By the end, he might or might not summarize what was said. Meanwhile, he will be interrupted countless times with questions, counterexamples, and arguments from the floor.

Americans will hardly listen to what the Frenchman is saying, because they don't know what he is talking about. "What is your point? Where are you going with this?" The French will not listen to the American presentation, because they will focus on one detail in the big picture and won't move forward until they can understand that specific point.

Avoiding Strategic Failures Due to Cultural Incompetence

The cultural dimensions presented earlier are valuable tools to all those who work in international settings. But you should be aware that they are the result of research aimed at quantifying an abstract and subjective concept—which is culture. As said before, culture is a complex and still abstract concept.

Researchers such as Hofstede, Trompenaars, Hall, and Lewis used quantitative methods to allocate scores to each cultural dimension. Although these scores enable us to compare countries and understand much more about different cultures, you would want to apply them either separately, or by combining them—which would be a more effective choice. Take those cultural dimensions as indicators of some facets, but not as a comprehensive truth about each culture. This will be your first wise choice when preparing your negotiation.

Negotiation is about strategic decisions. Successful negotiators have a pertinent strategy and know how to turn it into action. A good strategy is built on objectives that are clearly stated and guide the negotiators' path to reach them. But a well-designed strategy can fail because of cultural differences and misunderstandings. Negotiation strategies are not easily applicable from one country to another. So a successful strategy in one country may fail in another. Sometimes negotiators fail because their objectives are not realistic for that specific country, for example, in terms of timing. On other occasions, failures are due to strategic limitations, such as the team organization or a focus exclusively on price.

You now know about the main cultural dimensions, and tools you can use to understand your own culture first, and then your counterparts' cultures. Understanding your own culture is a very useful exercise. This makes you more aware of your values, habits, and reactions, and enables you to get some distance from what you take for granted. It also helps you to put yourself in your counterparts' shoes, to have a better view of how others can perceive you. You certainly noticed that some cultural dimensions as described by different authors are complementary, while others overlap. It gives you a more concrete idea of the broadness of the concept, and at the same time confirms the core aspects of culture.

Cultural incompetence means that the negotiator is not aware of the counterpart's cultural specificities or deliberately decides not to consider them in the negotiation strategy. This is typical in the case of negotiators who believe that business is just business wherever you are. As a result, they don't integrate culture when preparing their negotiation strategy and end up failing. To succeed in international settings, the negotiator should be culturally intelligent.

Using Cultural Intelligence (CQ) in Negotiation

The success of negotiating in an international environment requires managers to effectively communicate their messages in different cultural settings. Fisher and Ury (2011) state that a specific level of awareness, competence, and skill is required to navigate the relativity and complexity of the multicultural global workplace. Only a fundamental shift in mindset—and translation of this shift into new ways of working—enables negotiators to transcend the distance between them. The challenge is to build connections between what sets negotiators apart and leverage differences for better outcomes. Converting this into decisions and actions is the work of international negotiators with broader vision.

According to these authors, these are the five aspects required for cultural competence in international negotiations:

- *Open attitude*: Develop the openness of a global mindset to ensure receptivity to cross-cultural learning and to maintain a productive attitude toward difference.

- *Self-awareness*: Know and understand your own cultural preferences in values, beliefs, attitudes, and behaviors.
- *Other-awareness*: Recognize cultural values, beliefs, attitudes, and behaviors on your counterpart's side.
- *Cultural knowledge*: Understand other social and business cultures and be aware of how conflicts and problems are resolved and decisions made.
- *Cross-cultural skills*: Know how to translate your cultural awareness and knowledge into negotiation strategy and behavior.

Thomas et al. (2008) state that intelligence is fundamentally a scientific construct. This means it is not physically verifiable and has been notoriously difficult to define. Intelligence involves selecting and shaping the environmental context. The most well-known approach is IQ, which is a measurement of one's intellectual capabilities. *By definition, the outcome of culturally intelligent behavior is more effective intercultural interaction.*

Livermore (2010) adds that cultural intelligence (CQ) is an additional form of intelligence. In recent years, emotional intelligence (EQ) emerged as the measurement of one's ability to effectively lead socially and emotionally. Technical expertise is not enough. Negotiators work with people, and EQ helps assess the degree to which one is able to perceive, understand, and manage emotions.

Cultural intelligence picks up where EQ leaves off. CQ helps us to learn how to work effectively with people who come from different cultural orientations. Both IQ and EQ are universal measurements: they measure intellectual and emotional abilities in human beings independently of their cultures. In contrast, CQ measures human ability to cope with cultural differences.

A remarkable aspect of cultural intelligence is that everybody can develop it, unlike IQ and EQ. First, because it is a repertoire of skills. The primary emphasis of the CQ is to develop a skill set that can be applied to all kinds of cultural situations, which is nourished every day with your own intercultural experiences and understanding. Second, it is an inside-out approach. You must really believe. Interest and respect for your counterpart's culture has to be genuine. Cultural intelligence is a transformative model of cross-cultural behavior, not a list of dos and don'ts.

Cultural intelligence is a learned capability that builds on the other forms of intelligence needed by international negotiators. Just as they can expand their social, emotional, and technical skills, they can expand their ability to effectively negotiate across cultures. True cultural intelligence stems from within and transforms the way negotiators work with their international counterparts. Developing cultural intelligence is a never-ending process, as the outcomes from the actions (CQ action) stimulate negotiators' motivations (CQ drive) and another cycle starts over again.

In contrast to cultural *competence*, cultural *intelligence* is the ability to create and maintain a good relationship with very different people, in understanding their thinking patterns and specific way of life. Earley and Ang (2003) developed the concept of CQ based on contemporary theories of intelligence. Defined as an individual's ability to function and manage effectively in cultural diverse settings, CQ is a multidimensional construct targeted at situations involving cross-cultural interactions, which arise from differences in race, ethnicity, and nationality. Cultural intelligence is a specific form of intelligence, focused on the ability to grasp, reason, and behave effectively in situations characterized by cultural diversity (Ang et al. 2006).

Cultural intelligence is similar to other intelligences, because it is a set of capabilities rather than preferred ways of behaving (Mayer et al. 2000; Thomas et al. 2008). Thomas et al. (2008, 127) define cultural intelligence as "a system of interacting knowledge and skills, linked by cultural metacognition, that allows people do adapt to, select, and shape the cultural aspects of their environment." Thus, the development of cultural intelligence is composed of five stages: (1) reactivity to external stimuli, (2) recognition of other cultural norms, (3) accommodation of other cultural norms, (4) assimilation of diverse cultural norms, and (5) proactivity in cultural behavior.

Regardless of the cultural context, the objective in negotiations is for people to reach an agreement that satisfies their respective interests. Cross-cultural negotiation takes a great deal of CQ drive, requiring not only the motivation to do what is best for the *negotiator* but also for the *other party*. Effective negotiating also depends on CQ knowledge, as negotiators have to gain the necessary understanding to anticipate where the key differences may lie in the cultural systems and values involved. This understanding enables negotiators to use CQ strategy to develop a thoughtful plan for how to go about the negotiation process in a particular context.

The CQ model was initially created for international leadership. However, it is a valuable model for us because it has a number of specific characteristics relevant to international negotiation (Livermore 2010, 19). First, it is a meta-framework rooted in rigorous, academic research, which has been tested across multiple samples, time, and cultures. Second, it is based on research and modeled on the four-dimensional approach connected to the four aspects of intelligence (motivational, cognitive, meta-cognitive, and behavioral). Third, it is about more than just knowledge: it adds personal interests, strategic thinking, and resulting behavior to cultural understanding. Fourth, it emphasizes learned capabilities more than personality traits—which are more stable—and moves to human characteristics—which can be improved by training and learning. Fifth, CQ is not culturally specific, because it focuses on developing an overall repertoire of understanding, skills, and behaviors for making sense of the barrage of different cultures. The four dimensions are represented in Figure 2.7.

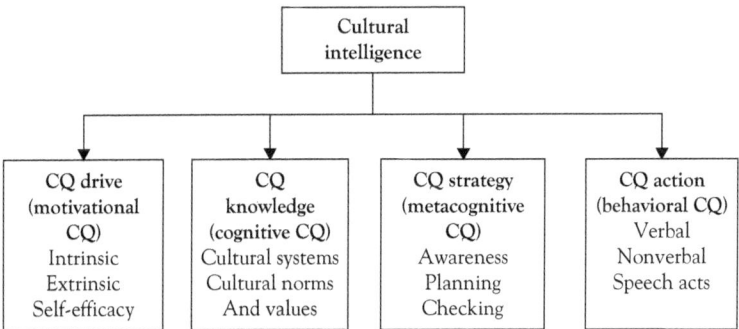

Figure 2.7 The cultural intelligence model

This model states that people with a high *CQ drive* are motivated to learn and to adapt to new and diverse cultural settings. *Cultural intelligence knowledge* helps to identify people who have a rich, well-organized understanding of culture and how it affects the ways people think and behave. *Cultural intelligence strategy* enables people to develop ways to use cultural understanding to develop a plan for new cross-cultural situations. *Cultural intelligence action* allows people to draw on the other three dimensions of CQ to translate their enhanced motivation, understanding, and planning into action.

Learning if and when it is appropriate to adapt your behavior to another culture is a complex question. It is more than just knowing the behavior of people from other cultures. It requires drawing on CQ knowledge and CQ strategy to anticipate what people from other cultures expect from you.

Develop your CQ by following the four steps:

- Step 1: Examine your motivations (CQ drive)
- Step 2: Seek to understand (CQ knowledge)
- Step 3: Think outside of the box as you plan (CQ strategy)
- Step 4: Effectively negotiate with respect (CQ action)

The cultural intelligence model is appropriate for international negotiations because it integrates the main drivers of the negotiation process: motivation, knowledge, strategy, and action. When using this model to prepare your negotiation, answer to the following questions:

- *CQ drive*: Why do I want to negotiate this deal? What are my expected outcomes? What are my other alternatives versus going through this specific negotiation? What will be the consequences of this negotiation for me if I succeed or fail? Where will this negotiation be a challenge to me?
- *CQ knowledge*: What is important to me? What would make me lose face? What would make me feel rewarded? How many people depend on me? What are the right and the wrong things to do? What should I know about my culture and my counterpart's culture?

- *CQ strategy*: How can I get what I want? Should I start building relationships before the negotiation starts? Should I build coalitions? How many people should I have involved in this negotiation? What aspects of our negotiation should I focus on first (offer, price, conditions…)? Which concessions can I offer? How can I talk about disagreements? How much time should I allocate to this negotiation? What is not acceptable to me, and how can I say that? Should I win even if I know that they will lose? Should I lose and preserve our relationship? How assertive should I be? Which alternatives can I mention?

- *CQ action*: Should I give gifts, and if so, which and how many? Should I invite my counterpart to a restaurant? Should I accept personal invitations? Should I talk about business during a social event? What should I do if it takes too long for them to make decisions? What should I do if they change the negotiators? What should I do if they propose something totally different? Should I call first and ask for an appointment? Should I accept any deal for the sake of our relationship? What should I do once the deal is signed?

Once you have answered all of these questions, you know where you are going, why, and how. Now try to do the same exercise about your counterpart. This will give you a better overview of the situations you might experience during the negotiation process.

Chapter FAQ

Why Do I Have to Adjust to Others' Cultures?

Actually, you don't need to adjust. You just need to be aware and show respect.

Focus on your negotiation goals and strategy. This is your job. Know about cultures so that you may get along well with your counterparts without feeling that your well-established values are being shaken.

You are not an interculturalist, and no one is expecting you to be an expert in cultural understanding. You are expected to be an intelligent international negotiator, who is culturally aware and able to integrate this awareness in a well-designed negotiation strategy and action.

Chapter Key Points

- Culture is a collective phenomenon.
- Negotiators' behaviors are function of their cultural norms and personality.
- Nonverbal communication conveys as much information as verbal messages.
- The use of translators is a double-edged sword, as they might override your leadership.
- Distant communication is tricky because it hides part of the messages and can convey inappropriate feelings.
- Culture should be part of your strategic thinking and preparation.
- Cultural intelligence includes motivations, knowledge, strategy, and actions, which combine to guide the negotiators' performance.

CHAPTER 3

International Negotiating Styles

International negotiation is about strategies, tactics, cultures, and styles. While it isn't true that each country has a specific negotiation style, there are some common aspects to the way people from the same country negotiate. Negotiation is a process composed of several steps and requires a lot of time to prepare before you arrive at the negotiating table. In this chapter, you will learn about the features of an international negotiation by walking through the whole process in integrating the cultural aspects.

The Negotiation Process

The most famous authors in the field of negotiation state that negotiation is a fact of life (Fisher and Ury 2011). It is a basic means of getting what you want from others. It is a back-and-forth communication designed to reach an agreement, when you and the other side have some interests that are shared and others that are opposed. People differ, and they use negotiation to handle their differences. In addition, some people will be easy to negotiate with and others will be difficult.

Here is the first aspect of negotiation that you should keep in mind. It is a systemic process composed of interdependent stages. Each stage must be consistent with the others to make sense and to be a real reflection of the negotiation strategy.

Negotiation is defined as a process by which two or more parties reach agreement on matters of common interest. All negotiations involve parties (people dealing with one another), issues (one or more matters to be resolved), alternatives (choices available to negotiators for each issue to be resolved), positions (defined response of the negotiator on a particular issue), and interest (underlying needs a negotiator has) (Cellich and Jain 2003).

Before getting to the core of the negotiation process, let's talk about the negotiation dilemmas.

Negotiation Dilemmas

When designing their strategies, negotiators go through several questions, doubts, and hesitation. What should be done? How? When? And what if …? The so-called negotiation dilemmas make negotiators think about the actions they should take and the consequences of doing them. There are five main negotiation dilemmas.

The Honesty Dilemma

The honesty dilemma has to do with how much you should tell your counterpart about your intentions, possibilities, and constraints. It is also about the type and amount of information to share with them.

On the one hand, giving too much information can be threatening, as they can take advantage of you. On the other hand, withholding information can result in negative consequences. This can be perceived as a lack of honesty and transparency, and you will be seen as an untrustworthy negotiator. As a result, when preparing your negotiation strategy, you should determine the type and amount of information you want to put on the table and measure the consequences of that choice.

It is worth noting that honesty and transparency are not the same concept, and neither are they universal. Honesty relates to lies or not telling the truth. In some cultures, lying is defined as saying the opposite of the truth, whereas in other cultures, omitting information is lying. So if you are *honest*, you are supposed to tell the truth; if you are *transparent*, you are supposed to tell *all* the truth.

One recommended technique is triangulating the truth. That means you need to check the information that was given to you by several other means. One of them is to keep asking your counterpart questions that relate to the information you need, and look for consistency. The Chinese use this technique at each interaction. Another approach is looking for other sources of information, such as other people who work with them, their direct reports, their website, information from their industry, and so forth (Malhotra and Bazerman 2008).

You also should be able to pick up on nonverbal communication to see whether or not it confirms what was said. In addition, you should watch for responses that don't answer your questions. Latin Americans often use this technique, either to avoid conflict or because they don't know the answer to your question and want avoid losing face by admitting this. It is the technique of creating a diversion to avoid the topic. It can also happen that the response you get is true, but it just doesn't answer your question. Ambiguity is part of the communication game in negotiation, and you need to be ready to cope with that. Finally, you can check reliability by asking questions about what you already know.

The Trust Dilemma

Without trust, you cannot do a deal. And trust is not given but earned. However, trust is not defined or built the same way in different cultures. In low-context cultures, for example, you earn trust from your counterparts by being objective, factual, and by not revisiting contract clauses once you have signed the document.

On the other hand, in high-context cultures, trust is dependent on people, and building relationships is the only way of earning it. Trust is needed for a negotiation to move forward, but you should measure how much trust you can have with someone, and how much you want them to feel they can trust you. Your counterparts will trust you if you are reliable. Reliability might be determined by your ability to tell the truth, be consistent and keep your promises.

Trust is a delicate thing. It requires a long time to build, yet you can blow it in a matter of minutes. All it takes is one incident of behaving inconsistently with what someone considers trustworthy behavior. It has to do with the relationship between pretrust—the belief that you will do what you say—and posttrust—the judgment about what you have done. If you go back on your word, you generate distrust (Blanchard 2013).

When you understand how your behaviors affect others, it's much easier to gain respect, earn trust, and accomplish mutual goals. Keep in

Table 3.1 ABCD trust model

Able	Believable	Connected	Dependable
Demonstrate competence	**Act with integrity**	**Care about others**	**Maintain reliability**
Get quality results Resolve problems Develop skills Be good at what you do Get experience Use skills to assist others Be the best at what you do	Keep confidences Admit when you are wrong Be honest Don't talk behind back Be sincere Be nonjudgmental Show respect	Listen well Praise others Show interest in others Share about yourself Work well with others Show empathy for others Ask for input	Do what you say you will do Be timely Be responsive Be organized Be accountable Follow up Be consistent

mind that people usually won't tell you that they don't trust you. You will need to deduce it based on their behavior.

The ABCD trust model is presented in Table 3.1 (Blanchard 2013).

One of the most convincing ways of motivating someone to do something is to use strategies that lead to early trust, particularly among multiactive and reactive negotiators. Societies can be divided into high-trust and low-trust categories. Members of high-trust cultures are usually linear-active. They assume that people will follow the rules and will trust a person until that person proves untrustworthy. By contrast, members of low-trust cultural groups are often reactives or multiactives. They initially are suspicious, and you must prove to them that you are trustworthy (Lewis 2006).

Research recently conducted with 173 participants from 26 countries demonstrated that trust is not a universal concept, as people can come up with several different definitions of it (Karsaklian 2013). Table 3.2 presents some quotes to illustrate this statement.

The Empathy Dilemma

A key factor about human interactions is that people tend to deny or project parts of themselves on other people. This means creating empathy is about building identification and avoiding denial. It is about

Table 3.2 Definitions of trust

Definitions of trust	Country
Trust is the feeling that you can rely on other people. We need some time to trust people here.	France
We can't easily trust someone, because people lie. People are very suspicious especially when it comes to money. No trust, money first.	Cameroon
It is a reliance on people's integrity, surety, and strength of a person. People who correspond to your expectations.	Morocco
Trust goes along with reputation and recommendation.	China
It is what allows you to have meaningful relationships with other people. It is the belief that the other person has your best interest at heart.	Canada
Belief that one can rely on someone else.	Sweden
Trust is sincerity. Trust relates to honesty: we should not lie or deceive others.	Japan
Reliance on and confidence in the truth. Trust covers themes such as loyalty and fairness.	Australia
Trust, but verify	Russia

demonstrating that you and your counterpart share something meaningful, so are able to walk together toward the fulfillment of your respective objectives.

Being empathetic is focusing on the feelings of the other person. It does *not* have to do with your emotions. Emotion is about *your* feelings; empathy is about the *other party*. If you are lucky and have a natural ability to empathize with people, you might get empathy quickly with your counterparts, thanks to shared values and some common ground. It will require less effort from both parties to feel a kind of belongingness and identification.

The Compete or Cooperate Dilemma

Negotiators who see negotiation as a competition have a hard time when their counterparts look for cooperation. Should you really choose one of them? Deals can hardly be totally cooperative, and one party may concede a bit more than the other one. Competition is inherent in negotiation but should not jeopardize the deal or the relationship. Cooperative competition is possible when negotiators establish objectives and rules together, so are connected by a process they both create.

The Strategy or Opportunity Dilemma

You have carefully done your homework and your negotiation strategy is well-designed. You have tried to foresee unexpected situations and are ready to get down to business. But some unexpected opportunities occur as you negotiate, and you want to take advantage of them. Should you really do that? How much risk would you take by deviating from your well-established strategy? How can you measure these risks? Negotiating is about risk taking, but you need to be aware of the consequences of capitalizing on appealing opportunities as they arise. It can be a tempting siren song.

The Role of Emotions in International Negotiation

You might have an angry person before you. It can be a genuine anger or just a tactic to make you feel frightened or angry, too. Don't try to stop them or to make them be reasonable at that moment. People who are feeling their emotions stop listening. If it is a genuine anger, people need to vent it. They will not hear a single word you say, as they are blinded by what upsets them. Let them say all they have to say. Once they calm down, you may start talking.

Take their anger seriously, and don't try to minimize what seems to be a relevant issue to them. It would sound like a lack of respect—or worse—like mockery to people who are emotionally shaken.

It would be better to help them release their anger, frustration, and other negative emotions. People get psychological release through the simple process of recounting their grievances to an attentive audience. When they are mad and you tell them to calm down, you devalue them—which makes them more emotional and perhaps even angrier.

Instead, listen to and commiserate with them, and they will calm down by themselves. They want to be listened to as an emotional payment. Don't avoid negative and stressful situations. Deal with them instead, if you don't want to increase frustration on the other side. But you should avoid expressing an emotional reaction to it. The consequences can be disastrous if you lose your temper, because emotions make people unpredictable. You can control your emotions but not those from others.

When your thoughts are driven by negative emotions, you are more likely to be anxious, defensive, and view the negotiation as a conflicting, stressful situation. You will be ready to attack instead of compromise. Your reasoning will be more emotional than rational, and you will lose sight of your objectives and might make hasty, poor decisions. Thus, you will be more likely to give up as the negotiation gets tougher, and as your goals begin to look unattainable. It is pointed out that anger can blind, fear can paralyze, and guilt can weaken. You'd better ask for a break or change to another topic, so that you and your counterparts can return to rationality (Ury 2008).

Your thoughts lead to your perception of the negotiation. What you see is not the truth, but your perception of it. This can be either positive or negative, depending upon your state of mind. Some people see financial crisis as a terrible threat. Some others see it as an opportunity. Many companies do much better during tough periods than when everything seems easy for everybody.

It is when things are getting tougher that you need to be more creative. The Chinese understand it very well. The Chinese word for crisis is WeiJi. This word in composed of two words: *Wei* means danger and *Ji* means opportunity. Each risky situation holds valuable opportunities ready to be seized by the people who see them. These are the positive thinkers. They take the best spots in the market while others spend time and energy just complaining about how bad things are. Make sure that your thinking supports your actions rather than pulls you down to mediocrity.

Human beings are reaction machines. The most natural thing they do when confronted with a difficult situation is to react—to act without thinking. It is noted that there are three common reactions: striking back (attacking right back or *attacking is the best defense*), giving in (just to be done with it), and breaking off (abandoning the negotiation). You should not engage in any of them. That is why you need to take rationality as your guide throughout the whole negotiation process. Rationality enables you to have a distant view of close things (Ury 2007).

Mastering your thoughts is mastering your emotions. If you are rational, you are objective and able to get perspective on the opportunities rising before you. Being overcome by emotions will blind you to opportunities, as your mind will be busy thinking how miserable you are, how badly the negotiation is going, and how far away you are from attaining your goals. You will take every single action from your counterpart as a personal attack. As a result, you will increase the size of the problem instead of looking for solutions to it. No problem is permanent or impossible to overcome. Solutions exist, but you must be able to see and use them. However, being optimistic is not enough. You must be able to see problems from different perspectives to find solutions to them.

To do so, you should know what you want and your ability to obtain it. The triangulation between what you want to *get*, what you *have to do*, and what you are *able to do* will show you what you are negotiating for. The want-have-able matrix represented in Figure 3.1 enables you to measure the power of your wants (motivations), your duties (constraints), and your ability to succeed in your negotiations. Ask yourself specific questions about the negotiation you are going to conduct. Insert your answers in the model on a scale of 1 (does not apply at all) to 10 (totally applies). Place a dot in the corresponding degree of the scale in each one of the three dimensions, and then connect them with a line. You will see in which sides the cloud is bigger and thus, more influential in your negotiation.

You are always in control of what your mind should focus on. To stay focused, your mind needs to be sure that you know where you are going. This clarity on your ideas and thoughts will prevent you from getting distracted with other factors that might naturally intervene, or be

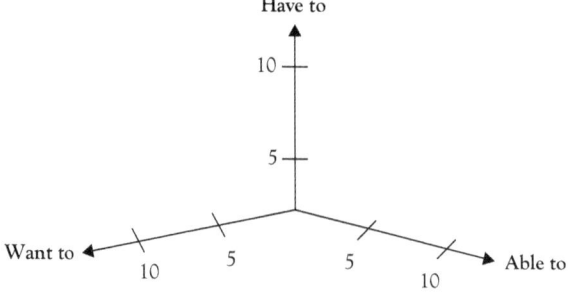

Figure 3.1 The want-have-able matrix
Source: Adapted from Krogerus and Tschäppeler (2011).

introduced by your counterpart. It will also avoid the periods of inactivity from your counterpart. If your counterparts use emotions just as a tactic to destabilize you, don't fall in that trap. Let them play their game. Keep your temper and carry on objectively. This is the best way of neutralizing their tactic. They will understand this does not work with you and will give up on it.

One of the worst feelings negotiators have is to feel stuck in the same stage of the negotiation. You need to know how and when to take action. You must make the negotiation evolve at each step. However, this evolution does not always rely on concessions, deals, or contracts. It can also be about building relationships, getting more information, getting more involved in your counterpart's life and building trust. Whatever it is, make sure that you are getting something worthwhile from each encounter. To do so, you need to understand the value of the intangible.

You are already wondering which types of cultures are more likely to use emotions in negotiation. You won't be surprised that multiactive and affective cultures use them. It's an easy way to lead people to do what they would not have done without this kind of emotional pressure. It might work very well when you know how to use it. However, the consequences can also be dramatic when the other side expresses regrets when it later understands that you have manipulated them. This may not be seen as fair play. Be very careful about using and facing emotions during negotiations, because they reduce information-processing abilities, which are critical in negotiation, and destabilize the situation. Use creativity instead of emotions.

Creativity is a key activity in international negotiation. It has been stated that creativity is the consideration of a wide variety of alternatives and criteria and the building of novel and useful ideas that were not originally part of the consideration set (Stahl et al. 2009). Because cultural differences are associated with differences in mental models, modes of perception, and approaches to problems, they are likely to provide strong inputs for creativity. If you are able to list new and old ideas by comparing them, the next step is to place them in the *thinking outside the box model* between chaos and order. You will then see the emergence of new and viable solutions, as represented in Figure 3.2.

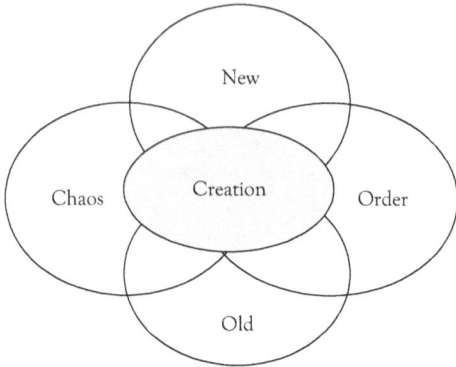

Figure 3.2 The thinking outside the box model
Source: Adapted from Krogerus and Tschäppeler (2011).

The Role of Attitudes in International Negotiation

Negotiators can be in different states of mind, such as happy, sad, depressed, puzzled, and so forth. Among these, he identifies four typical negotiating attitudes (Rich 2013):

- *Fusing*: This is the one who wants to combine the agendas of both sides to create a common currency for each participant. Fusers bring a positive, confident, and optimistic attitude to the negotiating table, without being intent on putting one over on the other side.
- *Using*: These people take advantage of the other side. They may bring confidence and self-confidence to the negotiation, but this comes at the expense of the other side's state of mind. They may be assertive and uncooperative, focusing on their own needs and not caring about their counterparts.
- *Losing*: Losers come to the negotiation with a defeatist attitude. Often this happens to satisfy the concerns of others.
- *Confusing*: These people labor under mistaken assumptions, misapprehensions, or prejudices, which may cause them to be losers or users.

Independent of their attitudes, never neglect your counterparts' problems. Their problems are your problems, because these can get in the way of the agreement you want. Listening to their problems and helping them to resolve these will move your negotiation forward more quickly, and you will be viewed favorably and appreciated by your counterparts.

Listening is the least expensive—and most valuable—concession you can make. We can say that you will have some credit to use with them after that. And, if you are unable to come up with a solution, you can bring more people to the negotiation who would (1) help them with their problems and (2) be your allies for the rest of the process. Your help will add to their well-being and they will be grateful. Do them a favor and they will owe you one.

From Preparation to Closing

If you fail to plan, you plan to fail.
    —Benjamin Franklin

You will go nowhere without a well-prepared negotiation. Preparation should take at least 70 percent of the time you allocate to your negotiation process altogether. This includes a number of steps:

- Get extensive information about your counterpart's company, market, and competitors.
- Analyze all alternatives—besides your offer—that your counterpart would have to satisfy the same needs.
- Know your company, products, market, and competitors very well. It is embarrassing when you learn about your own market from your counterpart. You look unprofessional and unreliable.
- Know about the people you are likely to interact with: their positions within the company, their reputation, their relationships with one another, their preferences, and dislikes.
- Know about your culture and the related stereotypes.
- Know about your counterpart's culture and create your own do and don't list.
- Establish your goals by creating your BATNA, your reservation price, and your potential ZOPA.

- List all the concessions you would be able to make and the ones you would find unacceptable.
- List all the concessions you expect your counterpart to make and the arguments you could use to persuade them to give you what you need.
- Choose your negotiation style and design your negotiation strategy.

Try to envision the whole negotiation process when you start preparing it. Think about the information you must have, the way you will use it, what your goals are, the strategies, and tactics you will need. Also consider concessions, closure, follow-up, and possible renegotiations. Think about the whole process, and then work backward. In other words, establish what you want to get and work through everything you need to get it. You can also draft an agreement and follow it to make sure that you are not forgetting anything important.

An effective way of having a good overview of your counterpart's business environment is performing a Porter's analysis. The five forces theory to industry structure was developed to help companies survive in a competitive environment. The five forces are (1) the threat of substitutes, (2) the threat of new entrants, (3) the bargaining power of suppliers, (4) the bargaining power of clients, and (5) the intensity of rivalry among competitors, as illustrated by Figure 3.3 (Porter 1980).

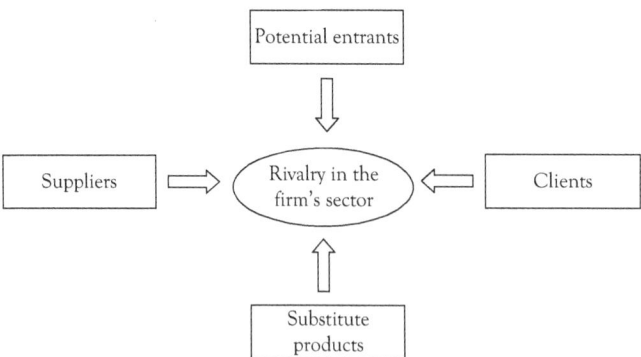

Figure 3.3 Porter's five forces model

You can fill in the bubbles with the information you get from your counterpart's market. Insert their competitors in the rivalry bubble in the center of the model and you will understand the types of pressure they face. Then list their suppliers and their clients, including you. The more companies you list on each side, the more bargaining power your counterpart has, and vice versa. Finally, assess the barriers to entry by identifying the potential competitors likely to enter the same market, and the alternative products your counterpart might have to satisfy the same types of needs. What your company offers also can be among the alternative products. This analysis of your counterparts' competitive situation enables you to identify their BATNA, and anticipate their objections to your arguments, which will be extremely useful to you in your negotiation.

In addition, surprise your counterparts by showing how much of their market you know, but avoid any sign of arrogance. You are not there to tell them about their job, but to help them to do it better. Never rely totally on their brief about their market, because it can be misleading for two main reasons. First, they might not disclose some relevant information because they believe it is proprietary. Second, they might have an incomplete or inaccurate perception of their own market.

Know the Market Better Than Your Counterpart

Consider the following situation. A director of an international company asks you to make a presentation to his clients over a lunch he organizes for his clients' enjoyment. Because there are a couple of topics you can speak to, you ask him to pick the most appropriate one for his clients. He chooses international negotiation. As an international negotiator, you are happy with that. You prepare your 30-minute presentation and fly to his country for that meeting. Nothing can go wrong, because you have mastered your topic, and the company's director knows his audience very well, as he organizes these events quarterly with different speakers.

Upon your arrival, he asks you to cut some of your slides to allow more time for questions. You would rather not do it. You know the reasons for creating those slides, but again, you think, "He knows his audience and this is the first time we are working together." Then you make your first concession by deleting the slides.

You give your presentation. Despite your enthusiasm and knowledge, the audience is attentive but there is little interaction. You finish early because there are not many questions from the floor. Why? They were mostly HR managers and not negotiators. Although they found it interesting, the topic wasn't connected with their day-to-day work life.

You realize you should have talked about other topics that you know well, such as intercultural management (which was among the topics you offered to your client and he did not pick). But should you show him that he has made a bad decision? Does he realize that he committed a strategic error in choosing the wrong topic? No, he does not. He would rather say that people would not have come if they weren't interested in the topic. Would you agree? And what if people would have come just for the networking, independently of the topic?

At the end of the day, everybody is disappointed. The participants would have rather attended a speech about something closer to their daily work lives. Your host, who paid for your trip, would have preferred to make his clients happy. And you, who had spent a lot of time preparing and traveling to deliver a presentation on a topic you have mastered, would have liked a more receptive audience.

Now that you have this experience, you know that: (1) you always need to check the information you are given, because often people say that they know more about something than they do; (2) in your follow-up, when you get back home, you already suggest some alternative ways of working together next time; and (3) he owes you a concession, and next time you work with him, he will be more willing to consider your advice.

Take your time to perform a Porter's analysis for your own company to have a better overview of your *own* competitive situation, too. But make sure that you see the markets as they are, that is, across physical boundaries. You are working in an international environment, so your analysis must not be bound to one country. Analyze all the possible alternatives of being part of your counterparts' competitive world, and not only his local market. The same applies to your company. If you focus on local competitors, suppliers, clients, potential entrants, and product alternatives, your analysis will be misleading. It will take you away from reality through a phenomenon called myopia.

Beware of Myopia That Can Lead to Negotiation Errors

Myopia is also an illness negotiators suffer from by being self-centered. Their preparation focuses only on how to persuade their counterpart to buy their product. Or, for the purchaser, how to make the seller accept their terms for the negotiations. People rarely take time to see beyond themselves. They don't know much about the other side, which is a paradox, because they will need the other side's participation to reach their goals.

This illustrates that preparing your negotiation is defending yourself against losing sight of your negotiation goals. The most common negotiation errors are the following (Cellich and Jain 2003):

- Unclear objectives
- Inadequate knowledge of the other party's goals
- An incorrect view of other party as an opponent
- Insufficient attention to the other party's concerns
- Lack of understanding of the other party's decision-making process
- No strategy for making concessions
- Too few alternatives and options prepared in advance
- Failure to take into account the competition factor
- Unskillful use of negotiation power
- Hasty calculations and decision making
- A poor sense of timing for closing the negotiations
- Poor listening habits
- Aiming too low
- Failure to create added value
- Not enough time
- Uncomfortable negotiations
- Overemphasizing the importance of price

Prepare Your Negotiation

The preparation stage of any negotiation is often overlooked, as people feel that they are too busy to invest time thinking about the deal in advance. Negotiators often are so sure that their strategy will work as well abroad as it has at home that they just take a few minutes to coordinate with the team members on the plane. This is also the moment when they read some tourist guides to learn a bit about the counterpart's culture before landing.

You understand that this is a very unrealistic and risky approach to international negotiation. When you are seriously preparing your negotiation strategy, start by asking yourself these questions:

- Who will be part of your team? Who *should* be part of your team? Do you need any experts? Which type of attitude do you want your team to bring to the negotiation?
- What roles are your team members going to play? Who is authorized to make concessions?
- Do you need any materials prepared in advance? Should you send some materials to the other side in advance?
- Where is the negotiation going to take place? Will you make presentations? How long should they take?
- Who is on the other team and how do they work? What do you know about them? Where did your information come from?
- Is there any history between your company and your counterparts'?
- What agenda will you create and how are you going to share it with your counterparts?
- What should you and your teammates know about your counterparts' culture?

You should make sure that you have all the needed people, each one with their specific competences and roles as negotiators. But other people than negotiators might intervene in some moment as experts. For example, engineers and lawyers are not trained to be business negotiators but their expertise is often needed in moments when the topics put on the table of negotiations become more technical.

In more deal-based cultures like the United States, negotiators talk about contracts from the beginning and to do so they take their lawyers to the table of negotiation at the very first round. This approach might be efficient when dealing with other contract-oriented cultures. However, it is not appreciated in relationship-based cultures. In these cultures, contracts and agreements are the last topic that negotiators talk about and it looks aggressive to bring attorneys from the start. It is perceived as a lack of trust in your counterparts and as if you were a contract hunter with no interest in building human relationship.

It is recommended that negotiators have a devil's advocate. This person's job is to criticize your decisions and find faults in your logic (Malhotra and Bazerman 2008). You will often miss some points in your strategy because it is *your strategy*. Even if you step back and try to get an objective look at your strategy, it is still your creation. Someone else, who is not involved in it, will have a different perception of it. The devil's advocate is not only useful for finding errors in what you have done, but also may highlight and confirm positive aspects of your strategy. Basically, you need a trustworthy, neutral person reviewing your strategy as an outsider to bring more clarity to it, thanks to an unbiased judgment.

Establish Your Goals

You need to feel that you are in control of *yourself* to be in control of *the negotiation*. If you have a clear idea of what you want and where you are going, you will feel much more confident. Make sure that you have listed everything that has to do with your negotiation, so you do not forget.

When you are writing down your negotiation strategy, first establish the different levels of goals you want to reach, and the factors influencing them—both positively and negatively. Then divide the factors into the ones you can control and the ones you can't. It's not worth spending time and energy trying to change what you cannot control. This will increase frustration and anxiety. You would be better served by focusing on the important items that you *can* control. Then you are able to make a difference.

You can even depict goals and factors in a situation and give them the needed importance as your negotiation evolves. Next to each controllable factor, write how and why you can use it. Next to every uncontrollable

Table 3.3 *Example of goals and controllable and uncontrollable factors*

Goals	Stage of the negotiation	Controllable factors and degree of influence	Uncontrollable factors and degree of influence	Your reaction to factors

Legend: ♦♦♦ crucial, ♦♦ strongly influential, ♦ influential, ◊ neutral, ◊◊ not influential

factor, write how you will deal with it. Give your scheme the shape you like. See the previous Table 3.3.

Making it clear what the negotiation is for will help you to persevere and overcome obstacles, because you are well prepared and know where you are going. Persistence is a key factor for your success. You need to be linear and objective to get what you want. But first you need to make sure that you are heading to the right place. Remember that efficiency is doing the right things, while effectiveness is doing things right.

Goals are the focus that drives a negotiation strategy (Lewiki et al. 2011). Determining the negotiation goals is the very first step in developing and executing a negotiation strategy. Then they can focus on how to achieve those goals. There are several types of goals negotiators may aim for: substantive goals (money), intangible goals (building relationships), and procedural goals (shaping the agenda).

Effective preparation for a negotiation includes listing all goals negotiators wish to achieve, prioritizing them, identifying potential multigoal packages, and evaluating possible trade-offs among multiple goals. The authors make it clear that wishes are not goals, and that your goals are often linked to the other party's goals. Effective goals must be concrete, specific, and measurable.

You should use a great deal of rigor to establish your goals. The Table of the Right Goal will help you to do that by using the *smart/pure/clean* attributes of your goals, as presented in Table 3.4.

Table 3.4 The table of right goals

S	Specific		The right goal	C	Challenging
M	Measurable	P	Positively stated	L	Legal
A	Attainable	U	Understood	E	Environmentally sound
R	Realistic	R	Relevant	A	Agreed
T	Time phased	E	Ethical	R	Recorded

Source: Adapted from Krogerus and Tschäppeler (2011).

Table 3.5 Example of goals you could have when using the table of the right goal

S	Quantities		The right goal	C	This is the first time we are working with these figures
M	Number of products	P	I suggest that you order # products	L	We have observed the legal aspects of our deal
A	Possible to produce	U	I understand that this quantity is appropriate to your needs	E	All parties will benefit from that
R	Possible to deliver by the deadline	R	This quantity will allow you to benefit from % discount	A	We have a formal agreement
T	In days/weeks/ months	E	I am giving you the best cost-efficiency ratio	R	We have a contract and we follow up

Let's assume that you are negotiating the quantities of products with a purchaser. Table 3.5 is an example of how to establish your goals for that round.

Use the goals portfolio matrix represented in Figure 3.4 to monitor the evolution of your negotiation toward achieving your goals. Establish your timeframe. Be realistic when doing this: it's not when you *want* it to happen, but how long it can *really take* to get you where you want to go, factoring in your counterpart's behavior. After each negotiation round, take your goals portfolio matrix and write down what you have achieved. First you need to list your goals, and then place them on the matrix. Some examples of goals in international negotiation are presented here.

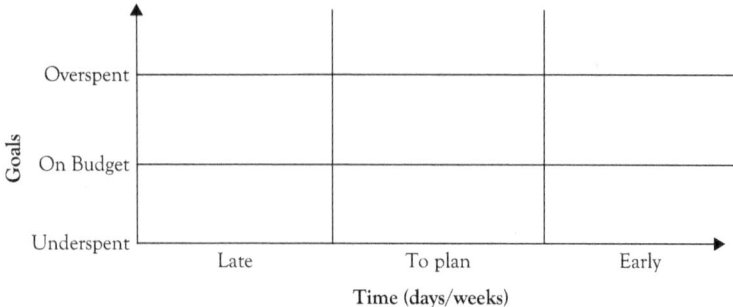

Figure 3.4 The goals portfolio matrix
Source: Adapted from Krogerus and Tschäppeler (2011).

List Your Goals and Then Place Them on the Matrix

1. Socializing
2. Getting to an agreement
3. Price figures
4. Delivery terms
5. Quantities
6. Gathering information

Here is an idea to consider. Sometimes, achieving the goal you have written down won't be the most important or rewarding part of a negotiation. Often it's the journey that matters. You walk side-by-side with your counterpart. If you don't reach your initial goals at some stage, you still need to be happy about the journey. In many cases, the journey itself should be your goal. It has to do with building relationships, earning trust, and gathering information. What can look like a waste of time in the short term can end up being the best way of succeeding a negotiation in the long term.

If you have not achieved what you wanted in some round of negotiations, that doesn't mean you failed. It can mean that your goal was not consistent with that particular stage of your negotiation, and that you needed more time and information to reach it. This also may mean that you will need to review some of your goals to make them more realistic and coherent with this stage of the negotiation process.

In other words, establishing negotiation goals is not enough. They should be realistic and attainable, and you should try to reach them—however you can get there. Sometimes it may take longer; sometimes it may go fast. This depends on several factors, such as the compatibility with your counterpart's goals, the evolution of the negotiation, your own and your counterpart's willingness to work together, and so forth.

Establish Your Strategy

In some situations, you will feel you are in a weak negotiating position. There is a common belief that sellers are always in a weaker position, as purchasers hold the power. As a purchaser from a French company once said, "We have our requirements and it is their (suppliers') job to take them into account." Sellers often forget to consider the switching costs to the buyer, and the intangible value of what they offer. They feel weaker because they are trapped in the price negotiation.

You can overcome this by leveraging your counterpart's weaknesses. It will be much easier for you to deal with the balance of power when you develop a SWOT analysis and are clearly aware of the strengths and weaknesses of all parties. Another way to minimize your weaknesses and to increase your strengths is building coalitions with other people who will bring the resources you are missing.

The SWOT analysis is based on a Stanford University study from the 1960s. This analyzed data from Fortune 500 companies and found a 35 percent discrepancy between the companies' objectives and what was actually implemented. The reasons for the difference were that the objectives were too ambiguous and that many employees were unaware of their own capabilities. Today, the SWOT analysis is an important tool for every person who needs to have a clear overview of the positive and negative aspects of their activities.

SWOT stands for strengths weaknesses, opportunities, and threats. It includes both internal and external factors. The strengths and weaknesses are internal factors that depend on the company's strategy and are totally controlled by it. They actually are consequences of the company's strategic choices. In contrast, the opportunities and threats are general tendencies generated by the market itself, over which companies have no control.

The strategic decisions based on a SWOT analysis aim at leading the company toward leveraging its strengths for taking market opportunities

Table 3.6 SWOT analysis

Your offer			
Strengths	**Weaknesses**	**Opportunities**	**Threats**
• Compatible with your client's needs • Uniqueness • Quality • Brand name • Company's reputation	• Obsolete technology • Lack of accuracy	• Legislation • Consumption habits	• Competition • Financial crisis

and reducing its weaknesses, to be protected from market threats. As for the Porter's analysis, don't forget that the markets you are analyzing are not limited by geographical boundaries. Table 3.6 depicts some potential aspects of your offer that you can include when performing a SWOT analysis.

The SWOT analysis can be used in several levels: for the company as a whole, one business unit, one line of products, one product, or even one person. Perform a SWOT analysis for yourself as a negotiator. Writing down your strengths and weaknesses will give you a clear overview of your abilities. Use Table 3.7 as an example.

Now focus on your strengths. If this comes naturally to you, then you are more likely to be confident, positive, and enjoyable. Use your strengths to leverage your actions as a negotiator and make a difference. In order to fully use them, you must be aware of them. More often than not, people are not conscious of their own strengths and weaknesses, and that is why they cannot identify opportunities and threats. Your strengths are your best assets, and you should rely on them. In addition, they will make you feel more motivated, and you will take negotiation as an enriching human interaction instead of the common classical perception: that it is stressful and confrontational.

When you believe you have done enough preparation, spare some time to rehearse. This may sound useless, or silly, or even appropriate only for junior negotiators. Think again. You will never know how long a presentation will take without rehearsing it, and you don't know how well your team will perform without putting it in a real-life negotiation

Table 3.7 Your personal SWOT analysis

Strengths	Weaknesses
Languages you can speak Ability to create empathy Cultural awareness Open-mindedness Technical skills	Fears Lack of cultural knowledge Lack of autonomy

situation. In addition, when you rehearse, you may think of some reactions from your counterpart that otherwise might not have occurred to you. As a result, you will look and be much more confident.

Meet Your Counterparts

Now that your preparation is done, you are ready to meet your counterpart. This is the so-called moment of truth. Whatever their culture, spend some time bonding with them. Try to find any common ground that could help you to empathize with them. Start building trust by showing that you have something to share. Build relationships by showing who you are, but avoid actions that could be interpreted as arrogant.

Negotiation is not just a technical problem-solving exercise. It's a political process in which different parties must participate and craft an agreement together. The process is just as important as the product (Ury 2007).

Negotiators come to the table because they need something from the other side. Your role is to create a favorable environment for both of you to work together and be productive. It's imperative that both sides feel comfortable and are in good spirits before getting started. Linear negotiators are just starting to understand and value what multiactives and reactives recognized thousands of years ago: investing in good long-term relationship.

There are several things to prepare before meeting your counterparts.

Agenda

The agenda for each meeting establishes what topics will be discussed, and in what order. You should reconcile your agenda with the one from your counterpart by making sure that critical issues are addressed. By doing so, the parties strengthen their confidence in each other. They are equally involved in decisions about the agenda, instead of one of them imposing it on the other. One important criterion to decide is the order of difficulty. Some negotiators might start with the easy topics to create a pleasant beginning and leave the tougher ones to the end. Others would rather get rid of the most complex issues at first and then move smoothly to easiest ones.

However, deciding on the contents and the order of the topics doesn't mean much in different cultures. Polychronic cultures have a more holistic view of the issues and will move back and forth across the subjects in the agenda. Moreover, what might be seen as peripheral in some cultures can be viewed as pivotal in others.

For example, Chinese negotiators find it relevant to present the history of the company and its founders' values, because the whole company draws on these values. If you are not patient enough to listen to that, you will not only be perceived as rude, but will also miss valuable information that will be extremely useful to you later in the negotiation. Establish an agenda that will lead you to your goals. Start the meeting with pleasant subjects, and create a collaborative feeling and atmosphere.

Some people confuse pleasant with humorous, and might start a meeting by telling jokes. This is a tricky way of breaking the ice. Humor doesn't travel well. You never know how jokes will be interpreted. If your joke requires translation, that will take all the fun out of it. In addition, some jokes are ironic or use stereotypes that your counterparts may perceive as humiliating or inappropriate. And how embarrassing is it when you tell a joke and your counterparts keep looking inexpressively at you? Instead of creating a pleasant environment, you are more likely to make everybody feel uncomfortable.

A classic example is the story of an American giving a speech in Japan. He is happy to see his audience nodding at everything he says, as the interpreter translates his words. He decides to close his speech with a joke. Before he has finished telling it, all the floor bursts into laughter. He is flattered and amazed and can't help going to see the interpreter to congratulate him. "You are so skilled," he says. "I know that translating jokes is not easy. You did it so well that people were laughing even before

I finished!" "Thank you," replies the interpreter. "It is very nice of you to congratulate me. But you should know that I did not translate anything. I just told the audience that our guest was going to tell a joke and that it would be polite to laugh."

Establishing a good working environment is not only necessary to get agreements, but also to get through disagreements. The best time to lay the foundation for a good relationship is *before* a problem arises. This allows you to create a more favorable environment to present your counterarguments and objections, without being aggressive (Ury 2007).

People should be receptive to what you say. But if the atmosphere is already tense, then every disagreement sounds aggressive, and counterparts are more likely to defend themselves than to listen to the other side and try to find solutions together. Don't attempt to separate substance and relationship, because this is not how people's minds work. What you say has more to do with you than with what you sell or buy.

Gather Information

While you are talking with your counterparts, try to gather relevant information that would be useful for you during the negotiation. Establish dialogue that allows each of you to ask questions and get answers directly from each other. Negotiation is more about asking than it is about telling. For instance, you may ask how they have been satisfying the need you are supposed to address, about their plans for expansion, the countries they envision reaching, and the ways they will do it (direct investment, alliances, etc.).

To make sure you get the information you need from your counterparts, first prepare a favorable environment for them to talk. Spend as much time as needed to *socialize* and get to know them. Let them get to know you, too. This phase of the negotiation is important, because it is also when you start creating empathy and building trust. You cannot work with someone who is a complete enigma to you. In addition, people don't give concessions to people they don't know. You can't make a request or present a proposal to someone with whom you have not established any kind of human relationship. Listen actively and acknowledge what was said. Everybody has a deep need to be understood.

Expressing agreement with the other side does not mean suppressing your differences. If you address these openly, it shows the other side that you understand their perspective, and they will welcome your arguments after that. Ury suggests that your counterpart will be positively surprised and might think, "This person actually seems to understand and appreciate my problem. Since almost no one else does, that means this person must be intelligent" (Ury 2007, 73). Then you have opened the door to show that you are, indeed, an intelligent international negotiator.

But realize that the other side will be aiming at gathering information from you as well. One traditional question when you are negotiating abroad is about how long you will stay in the country. Although it might sound just like a courtesy or curiosity question, it might represent important information for their strategy. In several relationship-oriented cultures, negotiators like to drag the other side out until their departure date by avoiding getting down to the core topics all over the time you spend there. They will wait until you are hurried to make you an offer that you might accept just not to go back home empty-handed.

Meeting Site

Decisions about the place to meet for the negotiation are strategic. Doing this on the home turf gives that negotiator a territorial advantage. It is psychologically more comfortable, practical for getting people involved, and gathering additional information—not to mention less costly.

If the meeting takes place in your country, you are responsible for making your counterpart's stay enjoyable. Think about their well-being in terms of accommodation, food, and visits. People who travel often need to feel comfortable when they are abroad. A bad night might put them in a very bad disposition to work the next day. The more you look after your counterparts, the better spirits you will put them in to work with you. In addition, they will feel valued and grateful and willing to reciprocate in some way.

Many people believe that negotiating in their counterparts' country puts them in a weaker position. This assumption has not proven true. Negotiating at your counterpart's place has several positive aspects, too. First, you may visit the facilities and verify statements they might make during the negotiation. Second, you can meet relevant people in addition to the negotiators, and you can get a sense of the company's atmosphere. Finally, because you invested in a trip, you made the very first concession. Your counterpart already owes you one.

However, there are some logistic aspects that you can't master if you negotiate at your counterpart's location. For example, if you need to make a PowerPoint presentation, ask your counterparts if they would agree for you to make a quick presentation at the beginning of your meeting. Follow-up to make sure that the equipment will be available, or bring your own. Don't forget to include that in the agenda.

Wherever the encounter takes place, be sure that there will be social events associated with work. Few negotiations are effectively conducted in meeting rooms and offices. Lunches, dinners, trips, shows, and karaoke are part of the whole process. Each culture has its own traditions, and you need to be ready to go along with them.

Your counterparts expect you to be an agreeable person, interesting to talk with about other topics beyond work. You should have some general knowledge and be able to discuss different subjects with different people. Nothing is more boring and disappointing than taking someone to a nice place to relax only to have them keep talking about work and deals. Your counterparts also want to know if they can have fun with you and spend pleasant time together. This can really make a difference when they are deciding between working with you or someone else.

You might argue that *socializing* does not look professional. But remember: negotiation is a human interaction more than anything else. It is imperative that your counterparts appreciate your human side. The more comfortable they feel, the more positive they will be about you and your business. Some negotiators do exactly the opposite. They want to make the other side feel uncomfortable, under pressure, and weak in order to take advantage of them. As an intelligent international negotiator, you want to take your counterparts to the negotiating table, not to a battleground.

Schedule

The time allocated to discuss each topic, as well as for breaks, does not mean much in several cultures. Time pressure is not always productive.

The amount of time depends on how many people participate in the negotiation and also on the questions. Be structured with linear-active counterparts, and flexible with multiactive and reactives. In any case, always be punctual. If possible, arrive early to check the meeting room and its facilities.

Now is the moment when you will use your list of concessions and demands. You and your counterpart will try to get what you both had planned during the preparation phase. There will be arguments and counterarguments. Depending on your counterpart's culture, this phase may be more or less time-consuming and might require a few or several rounds.

Master the Bargaining Phase

You know that it is impossible to reach any deal alone. Negotiation is a collective activity. There should be at least two parties to create a deal. The other parties have to be as involved in the process as you, if you want to work toward a deal. You have strings linking you to your counterpart. If each one of you pulls too hard, the string is more likely to break and both will be left with nothing. The classic image of the two donkeys linked by ropes and wanting to eat on their own sides at the same time is a good illustration of a negotiation, as represented in Figure 3.5.

Concessions and Reciprocating

Negotiators are often reluctant to make concessions because they think that is a sign of weakness. They believe that if you give a hand, next time they will ask you for the whole arm. This makes them afraid of not being in control of escalation. So when they make one concession, they expect their counterparts to immediately reciprocate. But there is a value attached to each concession.

If you want your counterpart to understand what a concession means to you—and what it should mean to them—then you need to label it. People tend to undervalue or ignore the concessions of others just to escape the obligation to reciprocate. Instead of simply giving something away, you should make it clear that your action has a cost to

Figure 3.5 The donkeys and the food

you, whether monetary or nonmonetary. Then it becomes embarrassing to your counterpart to justify nonreciprocity (Malhotra and Bazerman 2008).

However, make sure that all parties understand what reciprocating is supposed to mean. Even if the other side acknowledges your concession, they might still try to reciprocate with something of lower value. Your job is to eliminate all sources of ambiguity and state the level of reciprocity you expect. It is recommended that negotiators make contingent concessions, that is, that you explicitly tie your concessions to specific actions by the other party. Although this strategy may guaranty balanced concessions in your negotiation, it might reduce your opportunities for building trust, and developing and strengthening your relationship with your counterparts. They should be used at the right moment and for the right reasons. Do not overuse them.

Negotiation helps to create value through agreements that make both parties better off than they were before. Sometimes what you want to earn

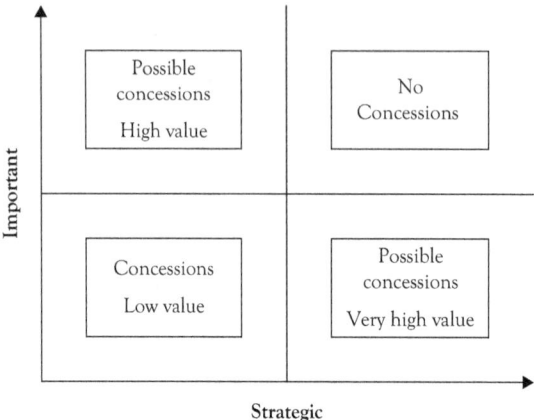

Figure 3.6 The importance × strategy matrix

from a negotiation is not vital to you. You could keep going alone, but it makes you better if you work together with a counterpart because this enhances performance and quality.

The Importance × Strategy Matrix represented in Figure 3.6 will help you to assess the value of each concession you might be able to make during your negotiations. There is a cell in which you will place every aspect of your negotiation that is not negotiable, because it is highly important and strategic. Very high-value concessions should be traded with other highly valuable concessions from your counterpart. The same is true for high-value concessions. Finally, you can play with the low-value concessions by using them at opportune moments throughout your negotiation.

Introducing New Ideas

If you are conducting your negotiation the way you wish—based on dialogue and mutual understanding—a new proposition should not come as a surprise. This will flow from the work you have been doing with your counterpart so far. The more what you present dovetails with your counterparts' interests, the easier it is to introduce new ideas.

Sometimes, it can be tough to convince the other side about the value of the alternative you are proposing. Remember that novelty can be frightening. People tend to stick to their well-known references and often are reluctant to change their habits and accept something that is totally new to them. They might argue that "we have never done it before," or "we have always done it this way."

Cultures with a high uncertainty avoidance index are the most reluctant about and suspicious of new ideas and about working with new people, too. Your job is to reassure them and make it easier for them to accept your new ideas by walking side-by-side with them throughout the process. But first they need to trust you. No other type of guarantee can replace the trust they have in you.

A very efficient way to get people to accept new ideas is to make them think they thought of them, as the French novelist Alphonse Daudet said in the nineteenth century: "La meilleure façon d'imposer une idée aux autres, c'est de leur faire croire qu'elle vient d'eux" (The best way to impose an idea to others is to make them believe it comes from them). This allows you to open the way for your counterparts to come up with an idea that matches the point you wanted to convince them about. Once they select an alternative, it becomes their idea.

The fact that we better accept our own ideas aligns with a well-known issue in international business, called the not invented here (NIH) syndrome. The NIH syndrome prevents people from buying imported products because they want to support local businesses, or because they don't trust the quality of foreign products. On the management level, the NIH syndrome creates tension between headquarters and local subsidiaries, because the local managers are reluctant to implement the decisions made by the headquarters without being able to adapt them to their particular market. Some intercompany negotiations happen because of the NIH syndrome, which end up having considerable impact on the company's international marketing strategies.

The Boston Consulting Group (BCG) matrix can help you make it easier to have your new suggestions accepted by your counterparts. This tool was developed at the BCG in the 1970s to assess the value of the investments in a company's portfolio. Each of the four cells has a specific name, based on the level of market growth and relative market share.

The items in each cell also can fall into four categories. The question marks have high growth potential but a low relative market share, because they represent new products, ideas, and concepts in a market. These need considerable financial support to develop awareness and value. The stars have a high market share and a high growth rate, but still require a lot of effort to become profitable and enjoy customers' support. The cash cows are former stars that benefit from customer preference and loyalty. They are the most profitable products for the company. Finally, the dogs have a low share in a saturated market and should not be kept in the long-term portfolio. The BCG box relates to the product life cycle with its four stages: launch (question mark), development (star), maturity (cash cow), and decline (dog).

You may use the same model, in Figure 3.7, for your new suggestions and arguments, since they have a limited lifespan, too. First, you present your new argument and face your counterpart's hesitation about accepting a novel idea. Then you prove its value for you both, search for their support, and ask for their agreement. Showing how your argument is valuable and unavoidable will create a need to the other side, and lead to acceptance. Finally, do not waste time and energy trying to convince your counterpart about the value of old arguments, which have already proven inefficient and no longer persuasive.

The BCG box enables you to introduce your arguments step-by-step. People are frightened when you present something that is perceived as being too big, too different, too fast, and too hard to achieve. Too much and too fast always sounds overwhelming. By taking an incremental

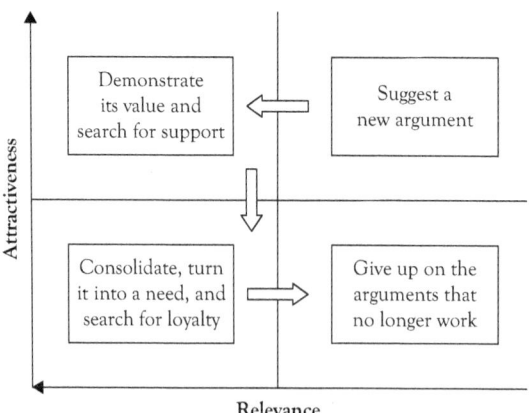

Figure 3.7 *The BCG matrix or the arguments' life cycle*

approach, you walk your counterpart through the whole process by anchoring each step. This reduces the distance between each anchor and the next, because big steps look much more risky.

To convince your counterparts about the value of your arguments, tell them what they wish to hear. Some facts and arguments can be presented differently, according to the needs of the people across from you. It is a matter of perception, which is, by the way, based on their personal values. For example, if you take Schwartz's model as an indicator, you will want to use a slower paced and reassuring approach with conservatives, while underscoring innovativeness to those who are open to change. You also should talk about how much your counterparts will gain by adopting your new arguments to self-enhancement-oriented people, or how much everyone would profit from the new idea to any self-transcendent people.

Dealing With Disagreements

Sometimes you will feel that bargaining is tougher, and you see that you are heading toward disagreement. Then you need to bring up potential losses instead of potential gains. At this point, your counterpart will be more open to hearing what you both will lose rather than what he can gain, because no one likes to lose something. This has nothing to do with threats, but with an objective analysis of what you both will miss if you don't reach an agreement. Use your power to focus your counterparts' attention on their own interest in avoiding the negative consequences of not agreeing to move forward.

When your counterpart only focuses on the negative aspects of your negotiation, you might be heading toward a lose-lose outcome. Talk about objective and factual consequences and not about what you will do if they don't agree. It is not about threatening them: it's about warning them and opening their eyes by projecting them into a future without the benefits of an agreement.

Consider the following situation. You have supplied your services to a foreign company for several years. You have recently been in a very successful partnership with them, working together for one of their clients. One day, that client calls and asks you to supply them with your services.

To ensure you are not being unfair to your partner, you ask the client if they want to work directly with you or via your partner. They say that they contacted your partner first, but the partner had proposed another supplier. Since the client had been very happy with your services, they wanted you to give them a proposal for a new project.

While you work on the proposal, your partner calls: upset because you should not be competing with them, since you are *their* supplier. You explain that they had chosen another supplier this time, and that you have the right to market your services as much as they do—mainly because the client requested this.

Your partner asks you to withdraw your proposal. They almost threaten you, because their company is larger than yours. You try to show them where you both are heading if they continue to behave in this way. You say, "We are competing with other companies. If the client sees that there is animosity between us, they will choose someone else." You propose a partnership as a solution. You say, "Then everybody wins, and I am sure that the client will select our common proposal."

Your partner does not accept. They want you to get out of their way. They try another tactic with you: using cultural differences as an excuse. They say you don't have the same understanding of the terms of your partnership, and that is why you should take yourself out of contention. "We know about our market," they say. Next, your partner tells the client that they should not consider your proposal. As a result, another company is hired to do the job and, just as you predicted, you and your former partner are out of the game.

Principled Negotiation

Knowing that some people run *from* conflict and others run *toward* it, arguing over positions produces unwise outcomes: it is inefficient and endangers an ongoing relationship (Fisher and Ury 2011). Negotiators tend to lock themselves into their positions. The more you defend your position and try to convince the other side, the more your ego becomes identified with your position. Then you end up trying to save your face rather than trying to get an agreement. It becomes a matter of honor instead of business.

There are four points that deal with the basic elements of negotiation and can be used under almost all circumstances (Fisher and Ury 2011):

- *People*: Separate people from the problem. Avoid being blind because of emotions.
- *Interests*: Focus on interests, not positions. A negotiating position often obscures the underlying interests.
- *Options*: Invent multiple options to find mutual gains before deciding what to do. Trying to decide in the presence of an adversary narrows your vision and inhibits creativity.
- *Criteria*: Insist that the result be based on some objective standard. Use fair factual and objective standards, such as market value, financial results, the law, and equal treatment—anything that can be used as a measuring stick that allows you to decide what would be a fair solution.

Note that standards might have limited impact on more implicit cultures, where perception plays a crucial role in interpreting facts and figures. In contrast, linear negotiators tend to stick to objective standards.

The principled negotiation's goal is to decide issues on their merits rather than through a haggling process focused on what each side says it will and won't do. This means that you look for mutual gains whenever possible. However, when your interests conflict, you should insist that the results be based on some fair standards that are independent of the will of either side. The method of principled negotiation is hard on merits, soft on the people. Table 3.8 presents the comparison between soft, hard, and principled negotiation (Fisher and Ury 2011).

One of the biggest mistakes a negotiator can make is to focus on trying to reconcile the *demands* of each party when they should focus on reconciling *interests*. While the demands can be incompatible, the underlying interests can be similar. In other words, negotiators should dig deeper to get to the interests instead of focusing only on the apparent demands. This strategy enables negotiators to have a broader view of the real problem and search for more creative solutions. It is even more important to dig deeper with counterparts from multiactive and reactive

Table 3.8 Principled negotiation and positional bargaining

Problem Positional bargaining: Which game should you play?		Solution Change the game: Negotiate on merits
Soft	**Hard**	**Principled**
Participants are friends. The goal is agreement.	Participants are adversaries. The goal is victory.	Participants are problem-solvers. The goal is a wise outcome, reached efficiently and amicably.
Make concessions to cultivate relationship. Be soft on the people and the problem. Trust others.	Demand concessions as a condition of the relationship. Be hard on the problem and the people. Distrust others.	*Separate the people from the problem.* Be soft on the people and hard on the problem. Proceed independent of trust.
Change your position easily. Make offers. Disclose your bottom line.	Dig in to your position. Make threats. Be misleading about your bottom line.	*Focus on interests, not positions.* Explore interests. Avoid having a bottom line.
Accept one-sided losses to reach agreement. Search for the single answer: the one *they* will accept.	Demand one-sided gains as the price of the agreement. Search for the single answer: the one *you* will accept.	*Invent options for mutual gain.* Develop multiple options to choose from; decide later.
Insist on agreement. Try to avoid a contest of wills. Yield to pressure.	Insist on your position. Try to win a contest of wills. Apply pressure.	*Insist on using objective criteria.* Try to reach a result based on standards independent of either side's will. Reason and be open to reason; yield to principle, not pressure.

cultures, as they tend to dissimulate their real interests by focusing more on relationship than on substance (Malhotra and Bazerman 2008).

Positive thinking gets help from the willingness to understand one another. People say that negotiation is about giving and taking. But when you give first, you are more likely to take more. If you show your genuine willingness to understand your counterpart first, they might reciprocate. This will make your interaction more pleasant and efficient, and you will move ahead faster. Being able to put yourself in your counterpart's shoes demonstrates that you are flexible, honest, and sincere. Also, once you have shown a willingness to understand their constraints and demands, you may more legitimately present your own difficulties and ask for their understanding.

Taking the first step forward is not showing weakness: it's showing willingness. You might get some pressure from your supervisor about having to be a tough negotiator. Sometimes you may be criticized for being *too nice* to your counterparts. Being willing to work together, being understanding, and making concessions is not being weak: it is being wise. As a tough negotiator, you are likely to get what you want faster and without making many concessions, but what you get won't last very long. It is a short-term strategy.

The long-term strategy is building things together with your counterpart. It is involving them in any decision you may make rather than imposing ways of deciding upon them. When people are associated with a decision, they feel committed and cannot walk away or disagree afterward. There is a personal involvement, because it becomes *our* decision instead of *my* decision. It creates bonds among people and high involvement throughout the negotiation process. This is the best way of creating standards to be followed by both parties. Because people hate to contradict themselves, they will be less likely to deviate from what was already agreed.

A good negotiator knows how to be flexible but firm. It means being objective and sincere without being aggressive. You can be tough but friendly. Being understanding and flexible does not mean that you are not firm in your commitments.

There is some confusion between flexibility and changing your mind. Being flexible does not mean that you change your mind every day just to go with the flow. It means that you are able to listen, analyze, and understand other standpoints. It means that you are intelligent. Once you have listened, analyzed, and understood, you can position your offer, make a commitment, and be firm about it. Better yet, you can legitimately ask your counterpart to do the same. Indeed, by making an exception, you create precedents you can use later.

In summary, focus on these four negotiation factors during the encounter: interests for reaching your goals, standards for resolving differences fairly, alternatives to negotiation, and proposals for agreement (Ury 2007).

When Negotiations Go Wrong

Working in situations where everything goes as you have predicted is easy but unrealistic. You should know how to negotiate in situations that can be very different from what you have imagined.

It is often annoying to have a demanding counterpart. Sometimes this feels like a never-ending negotiation, as your counterpart always asks for something more. This is like being nibbled to death by ducks. Instead of being upset by their demands, take these as opportunities to better negotiate. If they ask for more, you may ask for more, too.

This is the way people from several countries negotiate. Latin Americans and some Asians do not ask for everything at once. Just as their negotiating style is incremental, their demands are incremental, too. Once they get your initial agreement about one subject, they will wait to ask more about it bit by bit. You should also take into account their nonlinear perception of time. Because they mix past, present, and future, they see no point in asking for everything they need all at once.

The bargaining phase is over when both parties have agreed on several requests and are happy with the outcomes. Or the negotiation might also be over because no agreement was possible. In this case, the negotiators have few options: abandon the deal, ask for a mediator, and ask for arbitration.

Abandon means that both parties agree to give up on the negotiation, or one of the parties refuses to continue negotiating because it sees no possible deal. Mediation is a third-party negotiation in which one outsider will listen to both parties and help them to reach reconciliation. The mediator's main role is to take the parties back to objective analysis by showing the advantages for both parties in getting a deal done. Finally, arbitration occurs when one person makes a decision for the negotiators. In this case, the negotiators no longer have the option to decide and must abide by the decision made by the arbitrator.

The Jodari house, depicted in Figure 3.8, represents the role of the mediator if the negotiators are unable to see new solutions.

The Jodari House represents the need for creativity and open-mindedness in negotiation. There are only two rooms (Room 1 and Room 4) out of four in the house that you can see. Your counterpart can

Figure 3.8 The Jodari house

also see only two rooms (Room 2 and Room 1). You both have one room in common (Room 1) and that is a convenient way of starting your negotiation. As long as your negotiation evolves, you might want to expand the alternatives in trying to attract your counterpart to Room 4 by explaining the advantages of going there. But he cannot see Room 4 and would rather drag you to Room 2, which you cannot see and where you are reluctant to go. Then it becomes a matter of persuasion and the balance of power.

This picture perfectly illustrates the possibilities for negotiators: (1) one common ground to start negotiating, (2) alternatives that each can propose to the other, and (3) one existing alternative that they ignore because they cannot see it. While Room 3 is as much a part of the house as the three other rooms, it does not exist for the two negotiators because they cannot see it. It is a matter of perspective. Only a person placed on the other side of the house could see it is there. Ideally, the third person needs to have a higher view to be able to see the whole house. In addition, the picture represents how much of reality each negotiator can know. Reality and truth are one thing, and the other is how much people know about them. The difference explains the limited number of alternatives that individuals can see.

Ideally, the third person should be someone from your counterpart's network, with whom you will empathize. Their word has much more impact because there is already trust between them. In multiactive and reactive cultures, this is the only way of doing business. There should always be a third party—with a different but accurate view of the negotiation—whom they trust. Everything works via recommendation. You will need someone to open the doors for you and to help with supporting your arguments.

When positioning your offer, give one or two good reasons why your counterpart should agree with you. If you elaborate too much, they won't listen to them all and they will focus on the first ones. And the more you talk, the more you take risks, because what you say can also be used against you.

You always need to have some alternatives to keep the negotiation moving forward. Sometimes negotiators arrive at a deadlock and are unable to get out of it because they lack alternatives. If you are stuck in one point of your agenda, leave it and move to another one. You may come back when you have created better alternatives to suggest to your counterpart.

This is how polychronic people conduct negotiations, and you should feel comfortable with it. If you are to lead the negotiations, do it with your *conditions* and not with your *concessions*. Your conditions establish the tone and the pace of the negotiation. Your concessions allow you to move forward. Posit your conditions first and negotiate concessions after.

Not all negotiations are worth the time and effort you would allocate to them. You need to know when to give up on a negotiation and be happy with what you already earned. Walking away from a negotiation is not humiliating. *Au contraire*, it shows your counterpart that you know where you are going and that you are perfectly aware of the value of what you are negotiating.

The No Syndrome

No one likes to get negative responses, although *no* is still the word people hear most often in their everyday lives. While it is upsetting to get a negative answer, negotiators should see it as a new opportunity to improve their strategies. More often than not, negotiators think that the lowest price is all a client would ask for. Then they squeeze their offer to get the best price. By doing so, they often must cut features from their offer that would interest their clients and, as a result, their offer is rejected. If your offer is turned down, ask the client why this happened, so you can improve it for future negotiations. You will get very valuable information and will be very positively perceived by your counterparts because you are able to accept criticism positively.

If you don't want to have a flat *no* as an answer, ask questions for which the answer *cannot* be *no*. For instance, if you ask, "Do you agree with what I say?" it is easy for your counterpart to answer with a short *no*. Instead, ask, "How does what I say align with your expectations?" Then your counterparts will need to elaborate on their answers, and you will get more information to keep going with your arguments.

In addition, remember closed-ended questions are the last approach you should use to get information from counterparts in multiactive and reactive cultures. They might always answer positively, which will be misleading to you. They may not even answer your questions, and you will be trapped in their digressions without knowing how to get out of these and back on track.

Also consider that your counterparts may have limited power to make decisions or to deliver information, because they might have strict instructions not to do so from their hierarchy. Of course, this is more likely to happen in cultures where the power distance is strong. If you always ask them the same type of questions, you will always get the same answers. There are mechanical answers to well-expected questions. It is like pushing a button to turn a machine on and off. The result will always be the same. But if you ask your questions differently, and make it more of a conversation than an inquiry, your counterparts might be grateful because you are making their lives easier by opening other alternatives to avoid constraints.

Ask What Your Prospect Wants—and Then Listen

Never try to guess what a prospect wants. Instead, learn about their real needs and interests. A French company that specialized in training programs had to learn this the hard way. It was involved in a competition to earn a sizable contract for a program with a large organization in Belgium. The manager decided to design the offer by using two trainers. Each one was an expert in the different fields the project needed to cover.

During the presentation, the manager proudly presented their proposal by highlighting the extreme professionalism of the instructors who would handle the training. The potential client argued that, although their program was interesting, it was twice as expensive as what the other competitors offered. The French manager said that they could lower the price a bit, but could not match the other competitors because their offer was much better—thanks to the two experts. The potential client suggested the alternative of having only one trainer: a possibility the French company immediately rejected. They lost the deal. Why? They were so deeply persuaded about the superiority of their offer that they did not listen to their counterpart. What the Belgians wanted was to have only one trainer to give a quick overview of the topic to the participants.

Two years later, the same company was competing for a similar program for an institution of the French government. They designed a program with several trainers. They lost the deal again. Did they learn anything from those two failures? No. They were upset by the rejections and said that other providers were not serious, because one trainer cannot specialize in everything. The French company missed its prospects' point. They were not looking for great expertise in some fields. They wanted to provide their staff with an overview of a subject.

There are two lessons to learn from this. First, never try to guess what your client wants: know it instead. Second, what you consider a big value might not make sense to your prospect or client. People do not always search for the most sophisticated offer in the market. They just want to fulfill their needs.

In contrast, reducing features may also reduce value. You are lowering the value of your own offer without even trying to present it to your client. And when the client battles for a price reduction, both parties may end up dissatisfied. The seller loses, because the price and the offer were not as high as they were supposed to be. The buyer loses, because they will not be happy with the product's performance. The risk here is that the buyer might justify their own requests for a reduction by saying that the product did not satisfy their needs, and then look for another provider next time. Conversely, add-ons should really relate to qualities that add value to the client, not to your company.

Pay Attention to Your Counterpart's Negotiation Style

You will very quickly identify your counterparts' negotiation style by observing the way they reply to your arguments. If they are destructive and negative, they are playing the bad cop role (which is explained in the negotiation strategies section later in this chapter). If they are constructive and positive, they are playing the good cop role. You know how to play this game by using the good cop as an ally and by keeping your temper and never getting into a conflict with the bad cop.

As opposed to these two well-known behaviors in negotiation, negotiators tend to ignore the negative and constructive as well as the positive and destructive arguments, which is a strategic error. These types of replies provide you with precious information on what is appropriate or not about your arguments. That enables you to reorient your arguments in the right direction. Use the appreciative inquiry model in Figure 3.9 to help you to position your counterpart's responses.

Give undivided attention to what your counterparts criticize about your offer. This will give you the key to make them a new and more appropriate offer. When they explain the reasons why they reject your

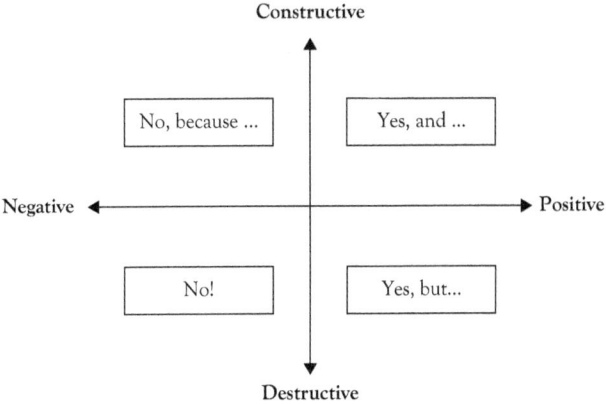

Figure 3.9 The appreciative inquiry model
Source: Adapted from Krogerus and Tschäppeler (2011).

arguments, they are keeping the door open for you to return with a more persuasive case. Take it as a chance to improve your performance as a negotiator and to come up with something that better suits your counterparts' needs.

Of course, the message will be conveyed differently, depending on the culture. In low-context cultures, your counterparts will tell you frankly and directly what is not acceptable in your arguments. But high-context cultures will use evasive and nonverbal communication for that. It is useless to ask them to be explicit. They can't and will avoid making you and them lose face by openly criticizing you. Remember, in high-context cultures, the person and the subject are considered the same, so any open criticism about the argument is taken personally.

You also need to consider the role of bluffing in negotiations. Linear negotiators rarely use it, because they consider this a waste of time and are more likely to put their cards on table. But multiactives might use it to see how far you will go to compromise and give them what they want. They might also do it because it is part of their tactics to destabilize you, or to measure your flexibility, or even to see how much you are on their side. Reactives are more likely to use constraints than bluffing.

Once again, during your preparation phase, determine what is negotiable and what is not. This is the best way of learning to say *no* at the right moment, when you see you are entering the walk-away zone. To have an overview of what is at stake in your negotiation, place challenges and risks in the negotiation zones graph in Figure 3.10. Make sure that you accept challenges with measured risks.

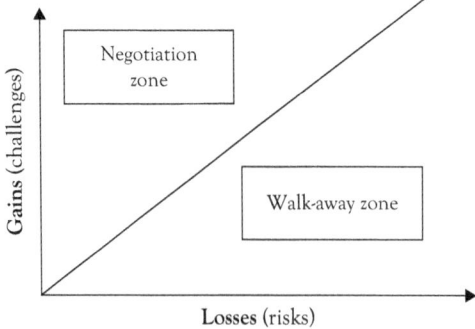

Figure 3.10 The negotiation zones

Tactics That Can Cause Upset

Another tactic used by negotiators to destabilize their counterparts is making them cool their heels in the waiting room. In most multiactive and highly hierarchical cultures, making others wait is a sign of importance and superiority. The one who does not hold the power should wait. The waiting time can vary from minutes to hours. If you are from a linear, nonhierarchical culture, you will perceive this as a lack of respect and professionalism and will be upset. Even worse, you might leave the room after a while and give up on the negotiation.

If you are an intelligent international negotiator, you will be prepared to this. First, you will not take other appointments on the same day or half day. Second, you will be psychologically prepared to wait. Any time earlier than you expected your counterpart to welcome you will be a bonus. Take some work or reading to do while you are waiting. It should be something that makes you feel like you are not wasting your time, but using it to do relevant things. Time will fly without you even noticing it, and you will be in a very good mood when your counterpart picks you up to start the meeting.

Here is another upsetting tactic. Your counterparts will start the meeting late but will not add any time onto the back end, instead saying they have another meeting to go to. Of course, you will not say that they can make the other people wait as long as you had to. Instead, say that you understand how busy they are, ask how much time you have, and show them that you are grateful to have the opportunity to tell them about your subject. Then present a teaser of your topic, apologize for rushing, tell them that you are at their disposal to answer further questions and offer explanations, and get ready to leave.

You will be surprised with the results. They may spend much more time with you than what they had announced at the beginning of your meeting, because they are curious about your teaser. Or they may get back to you very shortly, because they have tested you as an individual and a negotiator and admire your professionalism. They may even apologize for having made you wait for so long. Moreover, they know very well that you came over just to meet with them and how long you patiently waited just to have few minutes of their time. They are able to appreciate this without you having to tell them about it. Indeed, they expect people to complain about waiting and the short amount of time allocated to them, and show how upset they are about it. But as an intelligent international negotiator, you are changing the game in your favor.

Review Each of Your Rounds

It is imperative that after each day of negotiation, you do a debriefing with your teammates. Take a measure of what happened without judging anything. Just be descriptive and objective. Then compare what you got with what you intended to get. Assess the results and focus on the main takeaways. Make sure that you are aware of what happened, be it positive or negative. Shed light on what you got and what you could have gotten.

As you review the situation, clarify what you have achieved, what is left to do, and where you are going with your negotiation. Make sure that your actions and outcomes are consistent with your strategy and that you are not deviating from it. After each round, debrief by using the round review matrix in Figure 3.11. It enables you to compare your expectations with your outcomes and guides you in any reorientations you may need to consider before moving on to the next round.

Sometimes the gap between expectations and outcomes is due to the strategy itself, or to inappropriate actions you took. Other times, it can

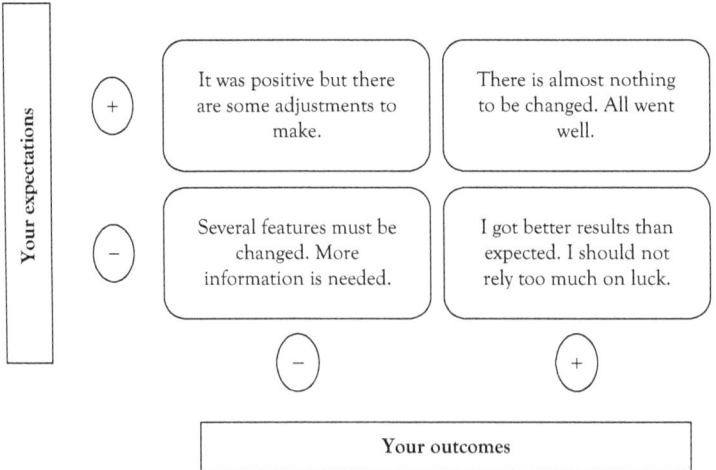

Figure 3.11 The round review matrix

Table 3.9 The learn-by-doing matrix

	Time 1	Time 2	Time 3	Time 4
Goals				
People involved				
Obstacles				
Successes				
What you learned				

Source: Adapted from Krogerus and Tschäppeler (2011).

be a matter of inconsistency between your goals and your ability to reach them in that situation. It's important to know the difference.

The best way of getting better as an international negotiator is to step back from what you have done and learn from it. After each negotiation, use the learn-by-doing matrix, in Table 3.9. Define a time frame, then write the goals you established, and how many of them you reached. Think about what you learned from the negotiation, which obstacles you needed to overcome and how. Consider the aspects of the negotiation in which you were successful, and the roles people played in the negotiation. This process will help you to keep preparing throughout the negotiation. Each round review will make you reconsider what you have prepared and make the needed adjustments to move your negotiation forward.

Having clear objectives and precise ideas of where you are going to will lead to successful negotiations. Your actions are consequences of your thoughts. Things do not just happen. Your thoughts change your actions. Each of your actions will lead to reactions from your counterpart, which in turn will trigger new actions from you.

This action–reaction process can create either a negative or a positive chain of events. The negative chain will draw on threats and revenge, and will pull you and your counterpart apart. It has to do with punishing each action with less flexibility. The positive chain will be constructive, and each action and reaction will add to building value together. It has to do with rewarding each positive action with new concessions. By being positive, you create a virtuous circle in which you and your counterpart negotiate by collaborating. It will take a lot of pressure off your negotiation, and your interactions will be much more pleasant.

Closing the Deal and the After-Deal

Often neglected by negotiators, closing a deal after reaching an agreement is the last but most critical part of any negotiation. When you close a deal, you are starting something new with your counterpart. You are saying hello and not goodbye. Some negotiators take the closing step of the negotiation process for granted. Once they have an agreement, memorandum or signed contract, negotiators stop attaching importance to the relationship with the other party. You should realize that signing a deal is not the end of a process but the beginning of something you worked hard to obtain.

Negotiators often forget that the purpose of making a deal is not to sign a contract, but rather to accomplish what the contract specifies. Reaching an agreement is one thing; implementing the agreement is another. Remember that you depend on each other to make things happen afterward. If you don't consider implementation throughout the negotiation process, you might end up not reaching your goals. Make sure that the agreement isn't only a signed piece of paper but a real commitment for all parties. You need to ensure that your counterparts carry out both the contract and the spirit of the agreement.

This is a main difference between low-context and high-context cultures, and also between linear and multiactive and reactive cultures. The main goal for low-context and linear negotiators is to have a signed contract. The whole negotiation process must take them there. After that, the counterparts go their separate ways and each one knows how to handle the work on their side.

In contrast, negotiators from high-context, multiactive, and reactive cultures see the contract just as an administrative formality for two reasons. First, they see the path to arrive at an agreement as just the first part of a collaboration. Signing anything more formal only means that they agree to work with you, and the serious work will now begin. Second, because they're nonlinear, they often review some clauses during the action plan. They find it natural to make some adjustments to the written contract as they put the words into action to fit new situations. You may feel as though your counterparts are niggling as they always have a little something else to ask you, whereas you think that the negotiation is over and don't want to start reviewing what was already said. This is just the way they get where they need to be with you.

You must be able to conclude your negotiation properly. First, you need to identify the closure moment. Negotiators are frequently tempted to keep the negotiation going by asking for more or reviewing what was already said. This is a very dangerous game to play. You get what you need during the bargaining phase. After that, you wrap up and leave the negotiation with what you received.

Bringing business negotiations to completion requires special skills and techniques. Negotiators must use their own judgment in selecting the most appropriate method to close the negotiations (Cellich and Jain 2003):

- Alternative: One party makes a final offer to the other side
- Assumption: The negotiator assumes that the other party is ready to agree
- Concession: The negotiator saves some last concessions to stimulate the counterpart to agree
- Incremental: Proceed by agreement on one issue after another from the agenda
- Linkage: Use the reciprocity approach and continue making mutual concessions until reaching consensus
- Prompting: The negotiator makes a final offer with special benefits if the offer is accepted immediately
- Summarizing: The negotiator sums up the key achievements of the negotiation and highlights the benefits for both parties if an agreement is reached
- Splitting the difference: Both parties are close to an agreement and the remaining issues are not relevant, so they close the negotiation instead of continuing discussions on minor details
- Trial: One party makes a proposal and the objections to the trial offer indicate how far they are from an agreement
- Ultimatum: One side forces the other to make a decision on the final offer

To conclude, summarize the main points you agreed upon, talk about a memorandum of agreement or contract, and, if possible, invite your counterpart to celebrate the agreement. But don't talk about it anymore. Just socialize and have fun.

Follow Up

Following up on a signed deal is paramount in the whole negotiation process but also often overlooked. In this moment, you show your counterpart that you are able to put into action what you promised in the negotiation. If things go wrong during this period, you are likely to lose your counterpart's trust and ruin your reputation. Information is quickly propagated throughout the market, so others might see you as an unreliable person, too.

Never forget to follow-up. When you are back in your office, call or e-mail your counterpart in a cordial way. It is not only about the contract or signing of an agreement but also about thanking them for their welcome, their time, or whatever positive and friendly aspects of your negotiation you can mention in the ensuing few days. Do it immediately after your encounter. If this isn't possible, never apologize for the delay by saying you were busy. That will make them feel devalued. They will believe that you have other priorities and just think of them when you have some spare time—even if this was not what you meant.

Remember: what you say is less relevant than what they hear. After this, keep in touch frequently. What the eyes cannot see the heart cannot feel. Show that you have strong links with them, and make sure they know that you care about and want to hear from them.

In one of your follow-up interactions, you will probably have a need to review some points of your agreement. Renegotiations happen more often than you think.

Renegotiations

Static agreements are unrealistic in today's ever-changing business environment. Too many uncontrollable and unpredictable factors happen and can lead negotiators to renegotiate their deals. Thus, intelligent international negotiators include potential renegotiation costs in the original offer to absorb these future expenses, which can be costly in time and money. There are some key points to remember (Cellich and Jain 2003):

Before the Contract Begins

- Consider negotiations as a dynamic process, requiring constant monitoring of the agreement.
- Build extra costs into the contract to cover future expenses related to renegotiations.
- Make the implementation phase an integral part of the overall negotiation strategy.
- Encourage a healthy relationship between the parties, as it is the best guarantee for a lasting agreement.

During the Contract

- Prepare for the possibility of renegotiations and maintain records of all transactions.
- Remember that agreements mean different things to different cultures, requiring flexibility, understanding, and patience.
- Do not blame the other party for any wrongdoing until you know all of the facts.
- Do not wait for minor problems to develop into major ones before considering renegotiations.

If Renegotiations Are Needed

- Before beginning renegotiations, consult with everyone involved in the original negotiation, as well as those responsible for implementation.
- Be sure you clearly understand the factors that trigger the reopening of negotiations.
- Foster constructive discussions between concerned parties, which is preferable to legal recourse.
- Keep long-term business objectives in mind when renegotiating.
- Encourage steps that ensure that all parties are satisfied to secure profits.

Negotiating Styles

Negotiators have their own personality, culture, and a specific way of negotiating. Some will ground their thoughts and arguments on past facts, others in the present, and others in the future. Use your energy to convince them in the way they find most appealing.

First, think about what drives your own thoughts and behaviors: is it the past, the present, or the future? Then analyze your counterparts' actions. If their arguments are more likely to be supported by past evidence, they are *memory-driven*. In this case, you will be more convincing if you ground your arguments on past facts and figures. If they are *dream-driven*, they will be more willing to hear about future projections of today's deals. Finally, if they are *reality-driven*, you would want to show them how beneficial it is for them to work with you right now.

Use Figure 3.12 to measure the proportions of time for each one of these approaches.

It was suggested that Europeans are memory-driven, as they tend to look for historical facts to explain current facts. Americans are dream-driven, by being a land of opportunities and future oriented. Asians are reality-driven, reflecting the industrialization of commerce in those countries (Krogerus and Tschäppeler 2011).

There are five main categories of negotiation styles (Cellich and Jain 2003):

- *Dodgers*: They don't like situations where decisions must be made and risks assumed. They try to postpone making a choice and avoid risk-taking situations.
- *Dreamers*: Their main goal is to preserve the relationship, even if it means giving up unnecessary concessions. They tend to agree with the counterpart and avoid being assertive.

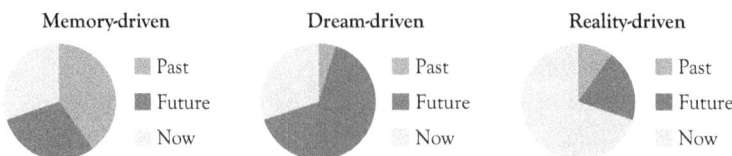

Figure 3.12 The energy model

Source: Adapted from Krogerus and Tschäppeler (2011).

- *Hagglers*: They view the negotiations as a give-and-take game. Persuasion, partial exchange of information, and manipulation dominate the discussion. They are characterized by a short-term outlook and quick movements.
- *Competitors*: They like conflict, feel comfortable with aggressive behavior, and employ hard tactics. They enjoy struggling to meet their objectives, even at the cost of alienating the other side, because satisfying their own needs is their primary goal.
- *Problem solvers*: They display creativity in finding mutually satisfying agreements. They take time to identify the underlying needs of the other party to explore how they can best meet their mutual interests. These people take into account substantive issues as well as relationship.

Despite the fact that it is unrealistic to generalize negotiating styles, some common aspects can be seen in negotiators belonging to the same culture.

Negotiating by Yourself or Negotiating in Teams?

In collective cultures, negotiators are more likely to be part of teams than to negotiate by themselves, which is characteristic of more individualistic countries. Also, in countries with high power distance, senior negotiators participate in the very first rounds as a sign of respect for the counterpart. In masculine countries, negotiators tend to be more assertive while in feminine countries they are more accommodating.

You might need to create a team of negotiators so you have a diverse set of abilities. This can increase creativity, and it conveys an image of strength and power. In addition, you feel less pressure because responsibilities are shared. Finally, your teammates can observe nonverbal clues from the other side while you are busy presenting arguments to your counterpart.

But working in teams can also lead to a lack of focus and consistency. It is important that one of the negotiators be appointed as leader, and each member has a specific role to play throughout the negotiation.

Be aware that any inconsistency or tension within your group can be sensed by your counterparts, who will use this to their advantage. These situations will increase the pressure you feel instead of the relief you get by sharing responsibilities with others.

Let's say you are negotiating abroad with your team. Your counterpart asks for a concession. Your teammate says yes and you say no. You see that this will lead to a trap, but your teammate does not. You try to dissimulate and take over the subject so your position will prevail. But your counterpart uses your colleague as an ally, addressing only him when talking and totally ignoring you. In some countries, counterparts will even try to manage you by creating an incident (spilling water or coffee, taking a visit to a facility, being called out of the meeting to talk to someone else in the company) to make you leave the room so that they can convince your teammate.

This can happen in any culture where negotiators don't put their cards on table. What can you do? Change the topic, or stop the negotiation by giving any excuse that will take you and your colleague out of that room to have a couple of minutes to talk privately.

Measuring and Taking Risks

The degree of uncertainty avoidance tells much about the willingness to take risks. Negotiators from low uncertainty avoidance countries take more risks than negotiators from high uncertainty avoidance ones. And the measures of risks can also be culture-dependent.

In linear cultures, negotiators tend to calculate probabilities of success and failure. In multiactive and reactive cultures, negotiators have a more qualitative and intuitive approach to measuring risks, which are based mainly on personal relationship and trust. Figure 3.13 demonstrates three

Deal-focused cultures	Moderately deal-focused cultures	Relationship-focused cultures
Nordic and Germanic Europe	Latin Europe	Arab World
Great Britain	Eastern Europe	Most of Africa
North America	Mediterranean region	Latin America
Australia and New Zealand	Hong Kong, Singapore	Most of Asia
South Africa		

Figure 3.13 Deal-focused and relationship-focused cultures

types of cultures according to whether their main focus is in on deals or relationship.

The categories presented here demonstrate what you should focus on when working with some of those cultures. In the deal-focused cultures, negotiators put their cards on the table and share information readily, because they believe that makes negotiation move forward faster. To them, the negotiation is over once the deal is signed.

In contrast, the relationship-oriented cultures invest a lot of time in building relationship and trust, getting to know you as an individual, and relying on a personal network. To them, a contract is just a written formality, and negotiations keep going along with the action plans.

Finally, the moderately deal-focused cultures require both objectivity and relationship building. Negotiators' reactions are less predictable because they move between two opposing ways of dealing with negotiation.

Here's a complication that often arises for international negotiators. *You* know about cultural differences and their impact on negotiation, but *your manager* does not. This means you are likely to experience some pressure from your manager to be a tough negotiator and get things done fast. Your company might ask you for short-term outcomes, while you know you need to build long-term relationships with your counterparts to get what you need. If you take an incremental approach, you may have both. You can get some short-term outcomes at each anchor, while you are building the long-term relationship.

Often international negotiators feel like the cheese in a sandwich between the cultures of their counterpart and their own company. They understand both but can hardly bring them together because, unlike him, the other parties don't understand that things happen differently in both cultures.

Cultural Schizophrenia or the Dual Personality Cultures

Using cultural dimensions to describe cultures can lead to the idea that they are stable and somehow predictable, thanks to general aspects common to all citizens. But this approach fails to take into account the fact that some cultures are highly influenced by others, so seem to have a dual personality.

For example, Indians are very mystic, implicit, and collective. But all of a sudden, they can switch to very goal-oriented behavior by asking direct questions and wanting accurate and immediate answers as part of the strong Anglo influence in the country. Other countries—such as Egypt, Lebanon, Mexico, Singapore, and Hong Kong—can have dual negotiation personalities as well. When negotiating with counterparts from these countries, you might be disturbed when they switch from one style to another very quickly, and several times during the same negotiation round.

Negotiating Strategies

There are two well-known types of negotiation strategies: win-win and win-lose. In the first, all parties should benefit from the negotiation outcomes, while in the second, only one party can win. People often forget to mention the third negotiation strategy, which is lose-lose. Surprising but real, counterparts might get to a negotiation with no intention of getting to an agreement. Let's see these in more detail.

Win-Win Strategy

As said earlier, win-win negotiations became the norm because they are politically correct. This means that your goal is to secure beneficial outcomes for all parties. If you chose this objective, you search for collaboration and are more likely to make concessions and avoid conflicts. It also means that you want to create good relationships with your counterpart, even if you don't get as much as you could out of that specific business. Your approach is more long-term oriented.

The win-win strategy relates to an integrative approach to negotiation. Objectives, constraints, and needs of all parties are integrated in the whole process. It also means that one party's problems become all parties' problems, to which a common solution should be found. By working together to find solutions to all parties' problems, the global gains are bigger and shared by everybody.

Table 3.10 A sample of definitions of fairness across countries

Definitions of fairness	Country
To be fair is to be neutral, without being biased. It is avoiding discrimination.	France
Deal with people with honesty, but people are getting greedy and don't care about sharing with others.	Morocco
It is being free from bias, dishonesty, and injustice. It is the conformity with rules and standards.	Canada
Free from favoritism, self-interests, or preference of judgment. Conformity with rules and standards.	United States
Honesty or justice. There is not such a word in the Swedish language.	Sweden
Mutual respect, equal chance, and equal competition. In a socialist country, we are used to cooperative enterprises, common ownership, and state ownership.	China
Everyone gets the same treatment and the same respect. But in Thailand we have double standards.	Thailand
We use this term when we don't deceive other people.	Japan
Decency, mateship, equity, unbiased, rightfulness.	Australia

What motivates negotiators to use win-win strategies is fairness. It is more about sharing than about dividing. You and your counterpart need to believe that your negotiation process and outcomes are fair for both. But just as for trust, fairness is not defined the same way in different cultures. Recent research demonstrated how different the perception of fairness could be across cultures, as described in Table 3.10 (Karsaklian 2013).

See the win-win strategy as a pot-luck dinner. Each party contributes with what they can bring, and all foods and drinks are put together and shared by all participants. In doing so, everybody has more to eat and drink in an enjoyable collaborative environment, and the organizer has a list of who brings what. This type of strategy is a good fit for universalistic, individualistic, low-context cultures, because they naturally share information, care about the community, and are objective in their requirements.

Win-Lose Strategy

Negotiators choosing this strategy don't believe that all parties can win, so they aim at protecting only their interests. Their rationale is that other people's problems are not *their* problems. They don't believe in transparency and sharing gains. They think that only one party can win, which implies the defeat of the other party. This strategy is a bit tricky, because the negotiation does not always look aggressive as it can be subtle. In addition, negotiators might announce win-win intentions but get into a win-lose strategy as the negotiation progresses.

Using the pot-luck dinner analogy, we can imagine a situation where each participant eats and drinks what he or she brought, instead of sharing with others. The party might be somewhat enjoyable, but there is less interaction and creativity because each person will stick with what she or he already knows and is used to, without being exposed to novelty. Participants might think since everybody does not bring the same amount of food and beverages, it would be unfair for them to share in what others have brought. As a result, participants would have exactly what they would have had for dinner if they had stayed home. Better yet, they will try to get some food from others without sharing their own.

It is a distributive approach because it divides people instead of bringing them together. This type of strategy is often used by collective, particularistic, and high-context cultures, in which people deserve different treatment according to the degree of familiarity and intimacy.

Lose-lose Strategy

It can happen that negotiators don't aim at working with their counterparts and cannot openly say so. They still might go to the negotiating table to play the game, but they will refuse all possibilities of agreement. No alternatives will ever be good enough. Lose-lose strategy leads to no outcome. Parties are unable to do business together.

Another possibility is that the negotiation starts with a win-win or a win-lose strategy and turns into a lose-lose one. Several factors can lead to confrontation, so each party says to the other, "If you don't give me what I want, I won't give to you." Back to the pot-luck dinner. One person would say, "If you don't bring the food, I won't bring the drinks" and they end up with no dinner at all. Often, lose-lose strategies require third-party mediation or arbitration.

Cultural adjustment aligns with the negotiation strategy; it depends on the balance of power. The one who adjusts the most is seen as needing the other more. In integrative negotiations, both parts are willing to adjust because the common goal is to get to a beneficial deal for all parties. But in distributive negotiations, one party will expect the other side to adapt more. Submitting the other party to cultural constraints is a way of increasing pressure and accelerating concessions and decision making.

Independently of negotiations, human nature can be more confrontational or more accommodating. Some people like provoking others, fighting passionately for their ideas and goals, versus others who run away from any conflict or aggressive situation. Culturally speaking, it has more do to with whose interests are to be protected and with how much we trust others.

In collective cultures, negotiators' responsibility is to defend the interests of their group instead of compromising with outsiders. On the other hand, in individualistic cultures, that responsibility does not exist, and compromising with the other party—who is not seen as an outsider—is more productive. It can also relate to universalism and particularism. Universalistic cultures aim at giving and obtaining the same things from any people they would be negotiating with, while particularistic cultures adjust their goals and strategies to the specific person they are negotiating with.

Conflicts of minor or major degree can emerge during negotiations, and you should be ready to face any of them.

Conflict Management

Conflict is the expression of differences in opinion or priority because of opposing needs or demands. People with diverse backgrounds and experiences hold different belief structures and values, which affect their prioritization, interpretation, and response to stimuli (Stahl et al. 2009).

The degree of conflict in a negotiation depends on the strategies used by the negotiators. The distributive strategy is more aggressive and can generate some conflict. Conflicts depend on the degree of assertiveness and cooperativeness, as shown in Figure 3.14 (Pruitt and Rubin 1986).

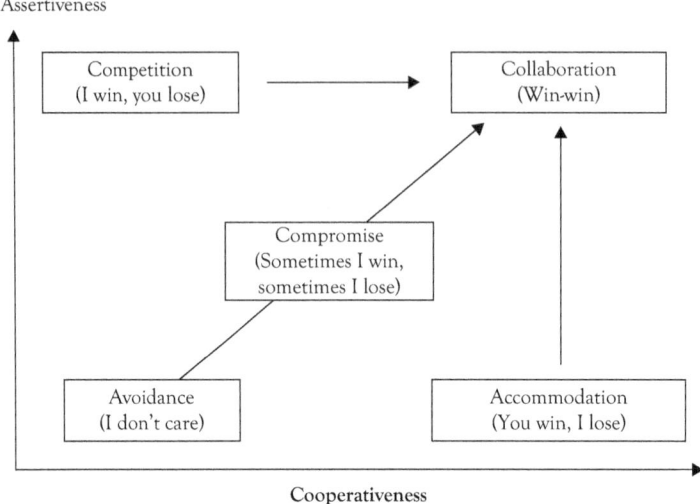

Figure 3.14 Conflict generation and management

Analyzing the negotiation strategies in the light of Figure 3.14, we would say that there are five types of strategies—but they all relate to win-win (collaboration) and win-lose (competition). The figure shows that no matter what situation you and your counterpart are in, you should make your way to collaboration.

Compromise and accommodation are often used in some countries. In cultures where the conception of time is not linear, negotiators tend to postpone their assertiveness, letting you win today so they have better opportunities to win next time. They might play the accommodation strategy to use their concessions as arguments to obtain others from you.

Compromise can also be part of the negotiation rules, and negotiators follow them by winning and letting others win. Finally, avoidance might seem simple to deal with, thanks to the low level of assertiveness. However, it's tougher to bring people together when some admit that there is a conflict and others deny it exists.

Conflict can be analyzed from the personality style's point of view, as follows (Diamond 2010):

- *Assertive*: The more aggressive you are, the more you try to meet your own goals at the expense of others, and the less you will get in a negotiation.

- *Collaborative*: Highly collaborative people tend to be more creative, look for joint gains, and search for items of unequal value to trade. That is, what is not of high value for you may be highly valued by your counterpart. They solve problems and see any problem as an opportunity.
- *Compromising*: Compromisers get less because they often pursue speed instead of quality. Busy people tend to be compromisers, as they take the first reasonable option and move on.
- *Avoiding*: High avoiders generally meet no one's goals. They don't engage, they avoid conflict, and, as a result, they get nothing.
- *Accommodating*: Accommodators tend to be great listeners, but they can go overboard in trying to reach a deal at the expense of their own goals.

These five styles could lead negotiators to the Three-A trap (Ury 2008). The first A stands for accommodation and reflects situations in which you say yes when you want to say no. That is, you protect the relationship even if it means sacrificing your key interests. This can be tricky, because it buys a temporary peace. After a while, you will regret having agreed because you did not really want to, and you might wish to take revenge for your dissatisfaction.

The second A stands for attack (assertive), in which you say no poorly. If accommodation is driven by fear, attack is driven by anger. You may want to punish your counterpart because of some behavior and so disagree with him in a harmful way. You use your power without concern for the relationship.

The third A is avoidance. This is when you say nothing at all. Because you are afraid of the other side's reaction, you say nothing in hopes that the problem will go away by itself. No solution can be found by you or your counterpart. You will never know what goes wrong on their side and will never let them know about what you think. There is frustration on both sides.

A recurring theme in international business studies is that problematic misunderstandings arise from cultural differences in styles of negotiating and handling conflicts. Several studies have analyzed East-West differences in negotiating by comparing U.S. managers to matched group in Asian society. Two patterns of findings have been observed repeatedly. Asian managers rely on a style of avoiding explicit discussion about the conflict, while U.S. managers are more inclined toward assertively competing with the other person to see who can convince the other of their preferred resolution of the conflict. Low concern for the opponent reveals two different styles: passively avoiding discussion of conflict as opposed to actively collaborating, and competing as opposed to accommodating (Morris et al. 1998).

Negotiating Tactics

A strategy is the overall plan to achieve the goals, which includes the action sequences that will lead to accomplishing these goals. Tactics and strategy often are confused. Tactics are short-term, adaptive moves that pursue higher levels strategies. Strategy is a broad, stable, long-term plan that indicates the direction for tactical behaviors. The most common tactics used by negotiators are presented next.

Deceptive

Negotiators play good cop, bad cop. You will face one negotiator who always agrees with you and reassures you (good cop) and another on the same team who always disagrees with you (bad cop). It is an effective way of making you deliver more information and respond about both the positive and the negative aspects of your offer. Some Asians might use these tactics.

Pressure

Your counterpart rushes you toward a decision. The last offer is usually used as a pressure strategy. It involves making you feel that if you don't accept their conditions now, you will miss a very good deal. This is your last chance to get it. Russians and negotiators from some Eastern European countries might use this tactic.

Oppressive

Your counterpart will demonstrate a high lack of flexibility. "Take it or leave it now." This means you are not likely to request something specific to your needs but to accept what you are offered. Again, Russians and negotiators from some Eastern European countries might use this tactic.

Emotional

Your counterparts will omit all objective arguments, instead stimulating your emotions. They will attempt to make you feel guilty, either because you are not making the concessions they ask you for, or because you are not accepting their arguments. Latin American negotiators might use this tactic.

Defensive

Your counterpart is evasive and does not answer your questions. You have serious difficulties in getting to the point and see that they always divert the conversation by changing the subject to get you distracted. Latin American negotiators might use this tactic.

Finally, you should consider the influence of governments and bureaucracy. Relationships between government and companies are country-dependent, and local laws align with local cultures. You should consider that, in several countries, a business negotiation integrates political negotiation. This means you first will need to negotiate with the government before getting to business with companies.

Different countries have different tax codes, labor laws, legal philosophies, and enforcement policies, and laws that influence any foreign investment in the country. Moreover, in some countries, government bureaucracy is deeply embedded in business affairs, and businesses are constantly required to secure government approval before they act. Sometimes you might think that decision making is taking too long and that your negotiation is not moving ahead as fast as you would like. Although it can be part of the other side's tactics, it also may result from the local bureaucracy. Being aware of it beforehand will prevent you from being upset, and then accusing your counterparts of deliberately slowing down the process.

Whatever your negotiation strategy and tactics, you will face the seven steps of international negotiation.

The Seven Steps of International Negotiation

Create Empathy

Find common ground and establish an immediate relationship with your counterpart.

Build Relationship

Dig deeper by building on common interests and values.

Earn Trust

Demonstrate honesty and reliability.

Create Value

Do this by showing outcomes and the benefits of the deal for all parties. *Use Time, Information, and Power*: Information is power, so the more you know, the better prepared you can be. Use and share information properly and in due time. Manage time instead of being managed by it. Control the negotiation pace by anticipating unexpected situations. Be realistic in calculating the time you need to get where you want to be. And understand that there is no such thing as a waste of time if you know how to use it in your favor.

Bargain

You know what you want to take and what you can give. If you give first, you earn a legitimate right to ask for concessions. Use a positive approach. Instead of saying, "If you don't, I don't," say, "If you do, I do," or even better, "I do, then you do."
Get the Deal: Never show triumph or relief when you sign a deal. This is just one more phase of a negotiation. Include your counterpart in the joy of a we-made-it-happen approach instead of an I-made-it one.

The Triangle of Power: Time, Information, and Trust

Power is a central factor in determining the outcomes of the negotiation process. Realize that power is not static and you should continuously assess and enhance it. In other words, sometimes you will hold the power during the negotiation, while at other times you will be in a weaker position. Never forget that information and opportunities may arise at any point.

The expression balance of power is very often used when people talk about negotiation. Power plays a very important role in all negotiations, and you need to know how to deal with it.

Power takes a number of different forms, as follows (Cellich and Jain 2003):

- *Reward power*: This is the ability to influence the behavior of another person by giving or taking away rewards.
- *Coercive power*: This is the ability to influence the behavior of another person by punishment.
- *Legitimate power*: This is the authority to demand obedience.
- *Referent power*: This is respect and admiration related to one's position or status.
- *Expert power*: This is attributable to a person's knowledge, skills, or abilities.

To have a clearer idea of how power can influence your negotiations, list its possible sources both for you and for your counterparts by using Table 3.11.

Nothing makes you more powerful than trust. The triangle of power in Figure 3.15 represents the role of information and time in building trust. When your counterparts understand that you have knowledge

Table 3.11 Sources of power

Sources of power	Yours	Theirs
Understanding the other party		
Knowing the competition		
Having expertise		
Having options and alternatives		
Setting the agenda		
Using home court advantage		
Having time		
Using listening and questioning skills		
Walking away/bottom line		
Being able to commit		

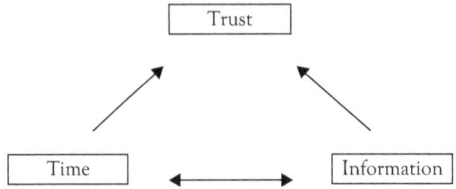

Figure 3.15 The triangle of power

thanks to information, that you deliver accurate data and that you share it with them, they will tend to trust you. Information is power—if you use it to develop your negotiation strategy and not if you hide it, which would be a source of distrust.

In addition, if you just use raw power, your counterparts will use their energy to defend themselves, instead of building something beneficial with you. If you manage time in a way that makes all parties feel comfortable without unnecessary pressure, you will enhance trust with your counterpart. Moreover, your counterparts will like to see you investing time in getting to know them and their culture.

Always set aside some time to visit your counterpart's country. It is useful for you to better know the country—as well as its culture. This also is flattering to your counterpart and demonstrates that you are not there just to *catch* a contract. Don't view it as a waste of time.

The Moderating Role of Effort in International Negotiation

Negotiating internationally requires more than information and time. It takes a lot of effort. Not only will you make the effort of collecting data and preparing your negotiation, but you also will make the effort of adjusting to several cultural environments and unfamiliar situations. Accepting differences is not natural to human beings, and it requires a great deal of effort to be tolerant. Also, you may need to make some effort to avoid being judgmental and getting upset by behaviors you would not naturally approve.

When you live in a world of cultural diversity, you need to cope with ideas and behaviors that don't make sense to you. Although it is important to be aware of them, you are not asked to accept them. Awareness is not understanding; understanding is not approving; and approving is not accepting. You just need to know about them to respect them. Respect is an expression of yourself and your values. You respect other people because you respect yourself.

There is a correlation between the success of your strategy and the amount of effort used in designing it. If you take shortcuts, the preparation may go faster, but your strategy could be incomplete. The effort you put into creating and implementing your strategy demonstrates your seriousness and professionalism as a negotiator, and it might lead you more surely to the deal, as illustrated by Figure 3.16.

The amount of effort you need depends on how specific you're willing to get. In other words, the more accurate and specific you are, the more targeted your effort will be. Having a specific focus helps you to avoid wasting time and energy, which is tiring, reduces your motivation, and ultimately is unprofitable. It's like swimming. You make a lot of effort when you swim against the flow and barely move forward. But when you swim with the flow, you move ahead quickly and smoothly.

Several decades ago, the Italian economist Vilfredo Pareto observed that the ratio in many economic activities was 80 percent of output for 20 percent of input. This has been confirmed in other business and non-business situations. This ratio became then the Pareto rule. You know now that only 20 percent of the time and energy that you spend in your negotiations will provide you with most of the outcomes you envision. Your job is to identify which 20 percent of your actions will be more likely to make your negotiation move forward, and then make them your priority.

Likewise, do not lose your temper if you think that you are wasting time in what appears to be meaningless interactions. These just might turn out to be the 20 percent you need to get to your 80 percent. In other words, 20 percent of high-value actions should enable you to reach

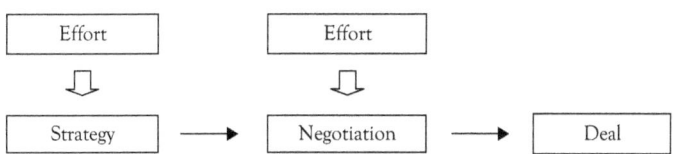

Figure 3.16 The influence of effort in negotiation

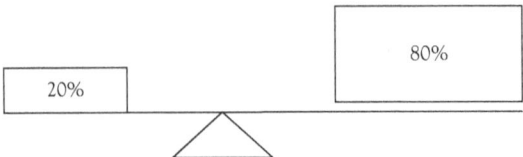

Figure 3.17 The Pareto principle
Source: Adapted from Krogerus and Tschäppeler (2011).

80 percent of your goals. The rest will represent the 80 percent of low-value actions, which are part of the overall transaction. Be ready to weigh your actions and concessions values accordingly. Use the Pareto principle in Figure 3.17 to better assess the type and amount of effort you need to be productive.

Using Silence and Other Disturbing Techniques

One confusing tactic is the use of silence. Asian cultures are naturally silent and accommodating. And ever since Asian negotiators realized that silence is disturbing to Western negotiators, their periods of silence have gotten more frequent and longer. You need to be patient and just wait until they break the silence themselves. If you feel uncomfortable with that, and talk more to break the silence, two things happen: (1) you give them much more information than what you will get and (2) you will look as though you are rushing them.

You already know that some cultures are neutral while others are affective. Neutral cultures might be disturbing to affective negotiators, because they cannot read their counterparts' facial expressions to know whether or not they are agreeing with what is being said.

Although some cultures are naturally neutral, others deliberately use the poker face to confuse their counterparts. Your job is to look for clues to understand their motivations and constraints. You need to identify their underlying needs. When Abraham Maslow came up with a theory of human needs in 1943, he stated that there are five levels that people want to satisfy, represented by what is known as the Maslow's hierarchy of needs (Maslow 1943). in Figure 3.18

By observing human behavior and evolution, Maslow identified a pyramid of needs, ranging from the most basic ones for survival—such as physiological and security needs—to more sophisticated and social

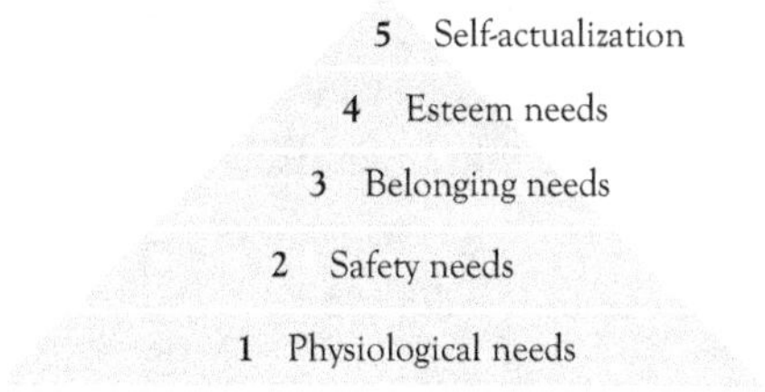

5   Self-actualization

4   Esteem needs

3   Belonging needs

2   Safety needs

1   Physiological needs

Figure 3.18 Maslow's hierarchy of needs

needs—including belonging to a group and being respected by its members. The highest level describes self-actualization needs, which motivate people to transcend barriers and move toward perfection by constantly striving to become a better person.

Maslow's typology has been applied to several disciplines, such as marketing, management, and, of course, negotiation. You should not miss the intangible motivations that drive your counterparts' behaviors. When you will identify your counterpart's needs, you must know how to deal with these to get what you need from them, as described in the following:

- *Achievement needs*: Help them to achieve their goals by walking all the way with them.
- *Security needs*: Reassure them by showing that they are making the right decision and how much they will benefit from it.
- *Belonging needs*: Make them feel part of an exclusive group by accepting your conditions. Show them that the two of you are on the same team.
- *Esteem needs*: Show respect by recognizing their expertise in their field.
- *Self-actualization needs*: Help them feel they are being open-minded people by accepting novelty and change, and transcending barriers.

For example, when your counterparts never stop presenting objections to your arguments, the best way to convince them is by rephrasing. Say something like, "If I understand—and please, correct me if I'm wrong—what you need is…" This way, your counterpart won't feel you challenged his authority or competencies. Then he may correct you by giving you additional information, which you will need to counter any objections. People need recognition, and showing openly that people are wrong, or that what they say is not relevant or pertinent, makes them lose face and compete instead of collaborate.

Chapter FAQ

What If I Don't Agree With Their Way of Doing Things?

You don't need to agree with others' cultural values to work together. You just need to respect them.

You should be aware of cultural differences to understand the manners of conduct.

Being aware is not understanding; understanding is not approving; and approving is not accepting.

You should know about their cultural behaviors—even if these don't make any sense to you, and if you don't approve the way they conduct their lives or accept their philosophy of life.

If you are judgmental about others' cultures, you might feel uncomfortable and thus be less productive, which your counterparts will sense. But, if they see that you are aware and respectful, they will perceive you as being professional and genuine. This makes it easier to earn trust.

Chapter Key Points

Here is a summary of the key negotiation factors recommended by Fisher and Ury:

- Negotiators are people first.
- Every negotiator has two kinds of interests: in the substance and in the relationship.
- Give your counterparts a stake in the outcome by making sure they participate in the process. Invite people to get involved in the process.

- Save face for all parties. Your actions should be consistent with their values.
- Recognize and understand emotions: yours and theirs. It's tough to separate fear from anger. Many emotions are driven by a core set of five interests: autonomy, appreciation, affiliation, role, and status.
- Communicate. Negotiation is a process of communicating back and forth for the purpose of reaching a joint decision. Listen actively and acknowledge what is being said. Leave enough room for your counterpart to talk.
- Build a working relationship. Get to know the people you will be working with and build a foundation of trust.
- Behind opposed positions lie shared and compatible interests, as well as conflicting ones. Ask *why*, but mainly ask *why not*. Each side has multiple interests.
- The most powerful interests are basic human needs: security, economic well-being, sense of belonging, recognition, and control over one's life. The purpose of negotiation is to serve your interests. If you want your counterpart to take your interests into account, explain your interests to them. Acknowledge their interests as part of the process.
- Put the problem before your answer. Create awareness, and then come up with a conclusion/solution.
- Be concrete but flexible. Know where you are going, but be open to fresh ideas.
- Don't search for the single answer. The first impediment to creative thinking is premature criticism, the second is premature closure. Separate inventing from deciding.
- Negotiate with objective criteria. Frame each issue as a joint search for objective criteria. Choose the most appropriate criteria and how they should be applied. Never yield to pressure: only to principle.

CHAPTER 4

The International Negotiators' Toolkit

You now have a number of models, graphs, and matrixes to help you to plan, operate, and monitor your international negotiations. In this last chapter, you will find the international negotiator's toolkit, which is a complementary set of tools to structure and organize your approach.

Sometimes you might feel uncomfortable with a negotiation. There are things that you want to do, but you don't dare take the leap to do them. An international negotiator cannot be shy or fearful. You need to enjoy each single negotiation round. If not, you are either doing the wrong job, or doing it the wrong way.

It can also happen that you hesitate too much before a tempting decision, and you are not conscious of what is restraining you. The rubber band effect will help you to identify the factors holding you back (your weaknesses) and the factors pulling you forward (your strengths). Listing these will give you a better overview of the situation, and you will be able to decide about allocating more weight to one of the sides. You need to know what is holding you back, and what would release you and let you work the way you would enjoy. Figure 4.1 suggests some examples of influential factors.

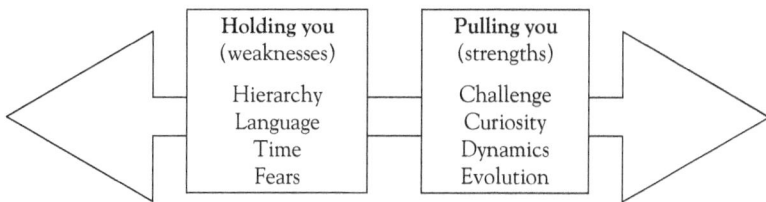

Figure 4.1 The rubber band effect

Source: Adapted from Krogerus and Tschäppeler (2011).

The Roadmap

International negotiators rarely visualize the negotiation process holistically. They are more likely to have a fragmented view of parts of it: some that are written and structured and others that are just in their minds. The negotiation flow scheme in Figure 4.2 gives you an overview of the whole process. It helps you to better prepare your negotiations and monitor each phase, so you can see where you are going.

People tend to say that negotiation is a stressful activity. It is true to some extent, because the outcomes are always unknown. There is a lot to be thought through and done before, during and after. The list of things you should think about is even longer when you work in international settings, which will add to your stress. You will want to get some of them out of your way by becoming accustomed to them beforehand. Here are some universal behaviors you can adopt in your day-to-day life, which will save you time and effort when you are negotiating abroad:

- Never interrupt people when they are talking.
- Never sit with your legs crossed in a way that others can see the soles of your shoes.

Figure 4.2 The negotiation flow

- Never point to something or someone.
- Never touch a child's head.
- Avoid putting business cards in your wallet or pocket immediately after you receive them.
- Accept invitations easily.
- Talk to people you don't know and build relationships.
- Try to pick up on nonverbal clues.

If you acquire those habits when you are at home, you won't need to think about any of them when you are negotiating abroad—they already will be part of your natural behavior. That will allow you to focus on your negotiation strategy—rather than avoiding making mistakes—increasing the time and energy you can devote to reaching your negotiation goals. You have too many core aspects of your negotiation to think about. The less time you devote to peripheral issues, the better you will feel.

The Intelligent International Negotiator

To be a better international negotiator, you should take into account the 10 cultural orientations and the four factors of the cultural intelligence model. The following table gives an overview of both.

Start by filling in the first column (cultural intelligence [CQ] drive) for each cultural orientation. This will allow you to understand your counterparts' motivations and the reasons why they will negotiate with you. Do the same thing in the second column (CQ knowledge). This helps you understand their values and norms, and what is likely to be acceptable to them and what is not. The third column (CQ strategy) will help you understand to what extent their values translate into their negotiation strategy. The last column (CQ action) will help you to picture their communication styles and the types of information they find useful.

Let's illustrate this in Table 4.1 by taking the French as an example of a culture you could negotiate with.

You can start by completing this table for your own culture. It will help you to know more about yourself and also to master the tool before you move smoothly to your counterparts' cultures.

Table 4.1 Cultural intelligence model and 10 cultural orientations

Cultural orientations	CQ drive	CQ knowledge	CQ strategy	CQ action
Environment	Constraint: would rather not do it but needs to	Constraints are part of life. Try to cope with them without making much effort	Try to benefit from the situation, as the negotiation was not a personal choice	Address the counterpart without demonstrating enthusiasm or strong inclinations
Time	Polychronic time: Semi-fluid slightly linear	Should take time to talk about what needs to be discussed, but patience is limited and should not miss opportunities	Use as much time as needed to get where they want to go. Deadlines are just guidelines	Take their time to make sure they have all the information they need to avoid risky decisions
Action	Being is more important than doing	Reputation, self-respect, superiority	Use titles and background to prove legitimacy	Focus on the person more than on the achievements
Communication	Middle context: Often subtle and between the lines, formal	It is rude to not mince words. Titles and formality are businesslike	Use second degree communication and expect others to pick up on the implications	Talkative: ask more questions than give answers. Often answer with another question
Space	Medium private space; large private life bubble	Closeness only when unavoidable. Private life is strongly protected	Keep distance, as the goal is not to make friends	Reluctant to talk about private life and to establish intimacy
Power	Strong hierarchy	Respect influential and important people	Important people deserve more attention	Need approval from the hierarchy, which can slow down the negotiation

(Continued)

Individualism	Individualistic and particularistic	Defend own interests but adapt behavior depending on the counterpart	The do and don't lists vary, depending upon the counterparts and the type of relationship established with them	Adapt discourse and approach depending on whom they are talking to
Competitiveness	Compete and cooperate	Compete without saying it openly, but would like to cooperate if possible	Competition is not politically correct. Should collaborate, but want to obtain more than counterparts	Try to find solutions for the counterpart if their problems are preventing them from finding acceptable conditions.
Structure	Order is not rigid	Switching quickly from topic to topic is being smart and intelligent	It is important to have clear ideas that can be used, depending on the situation and at the right moment	Might switch from one topic to another. Allow several digressions and associations with topics that don't seem to be related
Thinking	Inductive and systemic	Intellectual exercises are welcome. Intellectually skilled people can visualize relevant connections	No action can be undertaken without a long period of thinking and discussion	Every action has a reaction. Should be able to measure consequences of all possible decisions and anticipate all possible problems

International Negotiator's Toolkit

Here are several tools that will assist you in creating successful international negotiations.

You can start by identifying your own negotiating style by taking the following test.

What's Your Behavioral Style as a Negotiator Questionnaire

For each of the following statements, you have 10 points. Divide those points among the three possible responses to indicate what sounds most like you. There is no right or ideal score. Just remember to always use all 10 points for each statement.

1. **In preparation for a negotiation, you ...**
   a._____ Wonder what your counterpart will be like and hope you will not be taken advantage of in the negotiation process.
   b._____ Mentally prepare to compete with your counterpart and begin to plan your strategy.
   c._____ Cautiously prepare your case, making sure you have supporting data and research to strengthen your position.

2. **When initially meeting your counterpart, you ...**
   a._____ Take time to connect on a personal level and concern yourself with setting a positive tone before beginning the negotiation.
   b._____ Push to quickly present your goals, facts and data, having little need for social formalities before getting down to business.
   c._____ Begin the process slowly, listening to your counterpart's position before presenting your information.

3. **In presenting information during the negotiation, you ...**
   a._____ Want to make sure your counterparts know your concerns, but also know that you are concerned with their position.
   b._____ Present only information that will strengthen your position.
   c._____ Have a strong need to present all factual information in a detailed, sequential, and complete manner.

4. **When it is difficult to gain agreement on a point, you are likely to …**

   a._____ Compromise your position if it means you can get an agreement and preserve the relationship.

   b._____ Keep pursuing your options until you gain what you want.

   c._____ Ask questions to better understand your counterpart's position while continuing to present facts to support your position.

5. **When your counterpart surprises you with important information you did not have, you …**

   a._____ Feel that your trust has been violated.

   b._____ Quickly counter assertively with new information of your own.

   c._____ Examine the new information in detail.

6. **In trying to reach an outcome, at times you have …**

   a._____ Let the other party determine the outcome for the sake of reaching an agreement.

   b._____ Used the other party's weakness to your advantage.

   c._____ Not budged from your position if you believed that you were right and the other party was not being ethical.

7. **During the negotiation, your communication with the other party …**

   a._____ Is informal and not always related specifically to the negotiation.

   b._____ Is assertive, direct, and specific to the negotiation.

   c._____ Is cautious, reserved and unemotional.

8. **When a negotiation is not going well for you, you …**

   a._____ Get frustrated and begin to feel you are being personally taken advantage of.

   b._____ Focus on strategies you can use to achieve your desired outcome.

   c._____ Focus on the available facts and data and look for viable alternatives to help you achieve your desired outcome.

9. **When you need additional information from your counterpart, you ...**

    a._____ Worry that your counterpart will feel pressured or threatened by too many questions.

    b._____ Question your counterpart directly, targeting only specific information you need to be successful.

    c._____ Question your counterpart thoroughly to ensure the facts you have are complete and detailed.

10. **At the conclusion of the negotiation you ...**

    a._____ Care what your counterpart thinks about you and try hard to end the negotiation on a positive note.

    b._____ Are less concerned about what your counterpart thinks about you and more concerned about whether you have achieved your goals.

    c._____ Are concerned that your counterpart feels the final outcome was fair.

a._____ Total

b._____ Total

c._____ Total

Total = 100

If you've got higher score for **a**, your style is *amiable*, for **b**, you are a *driver*, or for **c**, you are an *analytical negotiator*. Here are the characteristics of each:

a Amiable	b Driver	c Analytical
Have a strong concern for relationships	Have a strong concern for outcomes; consider any relationship with the counterpart as secondary to the outcome or final result	Have a strong need for timely, accurate, detailed facts and information
Focus more on feelings and less on facts	Are focused more on facts, less on feelings	Are uncomfortable about bringing personal feelings into the negotiation
Have a need to be liked	Process information quickly; have little need for explanation or detail	Process information slowly

Ask many questions and may at times appear unfocused	Are impatient	Are economical
Are trusting	May view negotiating counterparts as adversaries	Can be emotional and difficult to read
Are typically good listeners	Have a strong need to win	Are logical and organized
Feel comfortable sharing personal issues and concerns	Are self-confident and assertive; may at times appear domineering and aggressive	Are highly principled
Work at a steady pace; don't like to be rushed		Speak slowly and directly; ask many questions
Have a strong desire for harmony		Are cautious and detail-oriented

Source: Stark and Flaherty (2003).

When you prepare your negotiation strategy, use the Cultural Analysis Grid to better understand your counterpart's cultural environment. It summarizes the most relevant information you should get before undertaking a negotiation.

Cultural Analysis Grid

Country:

Relevant history	(a) Key dates (b) Key events	
Geography	Location	
	Climate	
	Topography	
Social institutions	Family (a) Nuclear family (b) Extended family (c) Dynamics of the family (d) Female/male roles	
	Education (a) Primary education (b) Secondary education (c) Higher education (d) Literacy rate	
	Political system (a) Political structure (b) Political parties	

Social institutions	(c) Stability of government (d) Special taxes (e) Role of local government	
	Legal system (a) Judiciary system (b) Patents, trademarks…	
	Social organizations (a) Groups (b) Social classes (c) Clubs and associations (d) Race, ethnicity, subcultures	
	Business customs and practices	
Religion	(a) Doctrines and structures (b) Relationship with people (c) Prominent religions (d) Powerful and influential cults	
Aesthetics	(a) Visual arts (b) Music (c) Drama, ballet, opera (d) Folklore and relevant symbols	
Living Conditions	Diet and nutrition (a) Meat and vegetable consumption rates (b) Typical meals (c) Malnutrition rates (d) Foods available	
	Housing (a) Types of housing (b) Ownership and rental (c) One family or several	
	Clothing (a) National dress (b) Work dress-code	
	Recreation, sports, and leisure (a) Types available (b) Percentage of income spent	
	Social security and health care	
Language	(a) Official language(s) (b) Spoken and written languages (c) Dialects	

High- and Low-Context Country Orientation Table

Know what differentiates high-context and low-context cultures' negotiators, according to Hall, by using this table:

Factor	High-context culture	Low-context culture
Overtness of messages	Many covert and implicit messages, with use of metaphor and reading between the lines	Many overt and explicit messages that are simple and clear
Locus of control and attribution for failure	Internal locus of control and personal acceptance for failure	External locus of control and blame others for failure
Use of nonverbal communication	Much nonverbal communication	More focus on verbal communication than body language
Expression of reaction	Reserved, inward reactions	Visible, external, outward reactions
Cohesion and separation of groups	Strong distinction between in group and out group; strong sense of family	Flexible and open grouping patterns, changing as needed
Personal bonds	Strong bonds with affiliation to family and community	Fragile bonds between people, with little sense of loyalty
Level of commitment to relationships	High commitment to long-term relationships, with relationship more important than task	Low commitment to relationships, with task more important than relationships
Flexibility of time	Time is open and flexible, process is more important than product	Time is highly organized; product is more important than process

High- and Low-Context Culture Assessment

Assess your tendency to be from a high- or a low-context culture by using the following 10-point scale test:

I say what I mean						You need to read between the lines			
Truth is more important than politeness					Politeness is more important than truth				
It is important to contain emotions					It is important to show your human side				

I like a fast-moving discussion								I like a discussion with a measured pace	

I say what I want and then explain why								I explain the background before I say what I want	

I like an informal way of speaking								I like a formal way of speaking	

If your answers are more often on the *left side* of the scale, you tend to be from a low-context culture. The *right side* of the scale demonstrates a high-context culture's characteristics.

Linear-Active, Multiactive, and Reactive Culture Table

Know about the main characteristics of linear-active, multiactive, and reactive types of cultures, according to Lewis.

Linear-active	Multiactive	Reactive
Talks half the time	Talks most of the time	Listens most of the time
Does one thing at a time	Does several things at once	Reacts to partner's action
Plans ahead step by step	Plans grand outline only	Looks at general principles
Polite but direct	Emotional	Polite, indirect
Partly conceals feelings	Displays feelings	Conceals feelings
Confronts with logic	Confronts emotionally	Never confronts
Dislikes losing face	Has good excuses	Must not lose face
Rarely interrupts	Often Interrupts	Doesn't interrupt
Job-oriented	People-oriented	Very people-oriented
Uses mainly facts	Feelings before facts	Statements are promises
Truth before diplomacy	Flexible truth	Diplomacy over truth
Sometimes impatient	Impatient	Patient
Limited body language	Unlimited body language	Subtle body language
Respects officialdom	Seeks out key person	Uses connections
Separates the social and professional	Interweaves the social and professional	Connects the social and professional

Monochronic and Polychronic Management Style Table

Be able to identify monochronic and polychronic people by using the following table. Start by identifying your own time management style.

	Monochronic	Polychronic
Interpersonal relations	Subordinate to present schedule	Subordinate to interpersonal relations
Activity coordination	Appointment time is rigid	Appointment time is flexible
Task handling	One task at time	Several tasks are handled simultaneously
Breaks and personal time	Sacrosanct regardless of personal ties	Subordinate to personal ties
Temporal structure	Time is inflexible and tangible	Time is flexible and fluid
Separating work and personal time	Work time clearly separated from personal time	Work time is not clearly separate from personal time
Organizational perception	Activities are isolated from organization as a whole; tasks are measured by output in time (activity per hour or minute)	Activities are integrated into the organization as a whole; tasks are measured as part of the overall organizational goal

Cultural Compass Assessment

Know about your cultural profile by using this cultural compass assessment: Rank the following according to similarity to your own perspective 3 – most like me 2 – next most like me 1 – least like me:

1. _____ a. My decisions are primarily guided by what I have learned.

_____ b. I go with the flow and adapt my decisions to quickly changing circumstances

_____ c. When I make a decision, I focus on the result I am looking for.

2. _____ a. I tend to take each day as it comes.

_____ b. I tend to keep lists of tasks that I need to accomplish each day.

_____ c. In time, things do tend to work themselves out.

3. _____ a. It is hard for me to stop worrying about upcoming events or deadlines.

_____ b. Life has its own wisdom. Worrying is a waste of my energy.

_____ c. Let's focus on all that today brings, and take care of the rest one day at a time.

4. _____ a. We are meant to attend to nature's needs as much as to our own.

_____ b. Humanity's progress and survival depend on our control of natural resources.

_____ c. Nature's own power will determine our progress and survival; humanity's power can neither match it nor truly control it.

5. _____ a. In truth, we are much better off now that we can make more effective use of our natural resources.

_____ b. For all our great plans and projects, nature could put humankind in its place in an instant.

_____ c. "Effective use of natural resources" is the same as saying "exploitation of the natural world."

6. _____ a. No matter where you live, in the country or the city, there are a variety of forces operating that control your destiny.

_____ b. I strive to live simply, which is closer to the natural world.

_____ c. Modern conveniences actually help us appreciate the natural world.

7. _____ a. Developing my potential and my sense of self is the most important thing I can do with my life.

_____ b. Being alive and healthy is the most important thing to me; my accomplishments are secondary.

_____ c. It would be a waste if I did not achieve something important in my life.

8. _____ a. I prefer to relax and enjoy life as it comes.

_____ b. Peace of mind is possible regardless of external circumstances.

_____ c. I feel useless if I'm not doing something constructive with my time.

9. _____ a. Taking action is more important than commitment to a belief.

_____ b. We exist only in relation to other people.

_____ c. It is essential to be a good person; being a successful person is not the point.

10. _____ a. You have to be guided by what you think is right, even if you can't please everyone.

_____ b. It works best to have a good leader make the decisions; everyone should cooperate accordingly.

_____ c. Decisions affecting a group are more effective if everyone participates in the decision making.

11. _____ a. It is the individual I respect—not his or her position.

_____ b. Leaders of a group deserve respect because of their position.

_____ c. First and foremost comes unity; people who think of themselves first live at expense of others.

12. _____ a. The head of a group has to take responsibility for its success or failure.

_____ b. If someone in my group is having a problem, I am partially responsible for resolving it.

_____ c. I am accountable for my own success or failure.

Now score your individual culture compass. Place the number recorded beside each statement in the following appropriate space and add at the right. The highest number for each dimension indicates your preferred approach.

1a _____	+ 2c _____	+ 3b _____	= ____	Past
1b _____	+ 2a _____	+ 3c _____	= ____	Present
1c _____	+ 2b _____	+ 3a _____	= ____	Future
4c _____	+ 5b _____	+ 6a _____	= ____	Yielding
4a _____	+ 5c _____	+ 6b _____	= ____	Harmonious
4b _____	+ 5a _____	+ 6c _____	= ____	Controlling
7c _____	+ 8c _____	+ 9a _____	= ____	Doing
7b _____	+ 8a _____	+ 9c _____	= ____	Being
7a _____	+ 8b _____	+ 9b _____	= ____	Becoming
10a _____	+ 11a _____	+ 12c _____	= ____	Individual
10c _____	+ 11c _____	+ 12b _____	= ____	Mutual
10b _____	+ 11b _____	+ 12a _____	= ____	Ranked

Chapter FAQ

Will I Fail in a Negotiation If I Don't Take Cultural Differences Into Account?

The correlation between cultural awareness and adjustment and successful negotiation remains to be proven. Your intercultural understanding and flexibility just make your path to a better deal easier. Your counterparts will enjoy working with you because they perceive you as an intelligent professional and a genuine person who wants to share best practices with them.

Moreover, you will enjoy negotiating with people from other cultures much more if you feel comfortable in other settings in addition to your own culture. Taking cultural differences into account will make your life as an international negotiator easier. Don't try to *be* like the other party. All you need is to be yourself and be aware of whom your counterparts are.

This way, you create the favorable environment that is really important in international negotiations. But note that cultural awareness alone cannot predict positive negotiation outcomes. You need a well designed negotiation strategy.

Conclusion

In life, you don't get what you deserve, you get what you negotiate.

How often have you heard this? How closely associated are *deserving* and *negotiating*? Deserving is a reaction to an action. You have done something, so you deserve something. If you have done something good, you deserve to be rewarded. If you have done something wrong, you deserve to be punished.

Here is another truism: *In business you don't get what you deserve, you get what you negotiate.*

International negotiation is about action and reaction, too. If you are friendly, you will have a pleasant interaction with your counterparts. If you are aggressive, you will end up with a fight in your hands. If you respect others, you are respected. If you are honest, you earn trust. If your negotiation is well prepared, you will be successful.

Negotiation is not about winning or losing, it is about being successful. Successful negotiators manage information and people in a way that leads them to satisfactory outcomes.

This book tells you how to be an intelligent international negotiator. You are now able to plan your future negotiations by taking into account the key factors relating to culture, strategies, and tactics. By using the tools provided, you will get to your point very quickly and surely. You will design your negotiation strategies without neglecting crucial aspects of international negotiation. You will impress your counterparts with your knowledge, understanding, and open-mindedness.

Final Key Points

- Know what you want.
- Know about cultures, but know mainly about people.
- Don't try to adjust to another culture, but respect cultural specificities.

- Develop questioning, listening, and nonverbal communication skills.
- Use the appropriate language.
- Control your emotions and manage conflict.
- Bring people together and avoid being threatening.
- Make concessions with measured risks.
- Use critical elements: information, time, and power.
- Build bridges, not barriers.
- Be incremental: Walk side-by-side with your counterpart throughout the negotiation process.
- Be curious: Look for information and knowledge.
- Be rigorous: Make sure that you know where to go.
- Be human: Make the time to get to know people and to let them know you.
- Be professional: Demonstrate competence and technical skills.
- Be humble: Ask for advice from and learn with others.
- Have fun: Make a great human experience out of each negotiation.

Be yourself and keep in mind that you are working with other selves. You are expected to build value and not to change existing ones. Negotiation is above all a human interaction. It has to be an enjoyable and enriching experience for all parties. You should take it as a life experience in which you learn from others as much as you teach them.

Now you are ready to go. There is a whole fascinating world out there just waiting for you.

Safe travels!

References

Ang, S.; L. Van Dyne; and C. Koh. "Personality Correlates of the Four-Factor Model of Cultural Intelligence." *Group and Organization Management* 31, no. 1 (February 2006), pp. 100–123.

Blanchard, K. *Trust Works! Four Keys to Building Lasting Relationships.* London, UK: Harper Collins, 2013.

Cellich, C. and S.C. Jain. *Global Business Negotiations: A Practical Guide.* Stamford, CT: Thompson, 2003.

Diamond, S. *Getting More: How to Negotiate to Achieve Your Goals in the Real World.* New York, NY: Crown Business, 2010.

Earley, P.C. and S. Ang. S. *Cultural Intelligence: Individual Interactions Across Cultures.* Palo Alto, CA: Stanford University Press, 2003.

Fisher, R. and W. Ury. *Getting to Yes: Negotiating Agreement Without Giving In.* New York, NY: Penguin Books, 2011.

Hofstede, G. and G.J. Hofstede. *Cultures and Organizations: Software of the Mind.* New York, NY: McGraw-Hill, 2005.

Karsaklian, E. *In Brands We Trust. Competitive Paper: ANZMAC Annual Conference proceedings.* New Zealand, 2013.

Khakhar, P. and H.G. Rammal. "Culture and Business Networks: International business negotiations with Arab managers." *International Business Review* 22, no. 3 (June 2013), pp. 578–590.

Krogerus, M. and R. Tschäppeler. *The Decision Book: Fifty Models for Strategic Thinking.* London, UK: Profile Books, 2011.

Hall, E. *Beyond Culture.* New York, NY: Anchor, 1976.

House, R.J.; P.J. Hanges; M. Javidan; P.W. Dorfman; and V. Gupta. *Culture, Leadership and Organizations. The GLOBE Study of 62 Societies.* Sage, U.S.: 2004.

Lewiki, R.; D.M. Sauders; and B. Barry. *Essentials of Negotiation.* New York, NY: McGraw-Hill International edition, 2011.

Lewis, R. D. *When Teams Collide: Managing the International Team Successfully.* London, UK and Boston, MA: Nicholas Brealey, 2012.

Lewis, R. D. *When Cultures Collide: Leading Across Cultures.* London, UK and Boston, MA: Nicholas Brealey, 2006.

Livermore, D. *Leading with Cultural Intelligence: The New Secret to Success.* New York, NY: AMACOM, 2010.

Malhotra, D. and M.H. Bazerman. *Negotiation Genius.* New York, NY: Bantam Books, 2008.

Maslow, A. H. "A Theory of Human Motivation." *Psychological Review* 50, no. 4 (July 1943), pp. 370–96.

Morris, M.W.; K.Y. Williams; K. Leung; and R. Larrick. "Conflict Management Style: Accounting for Cross-National Differences." *Journal of International Business Studies* 29, no. 4 (Fourth Quarter 1998), pp. 729–747.

Porter, M. *Competitive Advantage: Creating and Sustaining Superior Performance.* New York, NY: Free Press, 1980.

Pruitt, D. and J.F. Rubin. *Social Conflict: Escalation, Stalemate and Settlement.* New York, NY: Random, 1986.

Rich, C. *The Yes Book: The Art of Negotiation.* London, UK: Virgin Books

Schwartz, S.H. and W. Bilsky. "Toward a Universal Psychological Structure of Human Values." *Journal of Personality and Social Psychology* 53, no. 3 (January 1987), pp. 550–562.

Stahl, G.; M.L. Maznevski; A. Voigt; and K. Jonsen. "Unraveling the Effects of Cultural Diversity in Deams: A meta-analysis of research on multicultural work groups." *Journal of International Business Studies* 40, (July 2009), pp. 1–20.

Stark, P.B. and Flaherty, J. *The Only Negotiating Guide You'll Ever Need.* New York, NY: Crown Press, 2003.

Thomas, D.C.; E. Elron; G. Stahl; B.Z. Ekelund; E.R. Ravlin; J.L. Cerdin; S. Poelmans; R. Brislin; A. Pekerti; Z. Aycan; M. Maznevski; K. Au; and M. Lazarova. "Cultural Intelligence: Domain and Assessment." *International Journal of Cross Cultural Management* 8, no. 2 (August 2008), pp. 123–143.

Triandis, H.C. "Cultural Intelligence in Organizations." *Group and Organization Management* 31, no. 1 (February 2006), pp. 20–27.

Trompenaars, F. and C. Hampden-Turner. *Riding the Waves of Culture: Understanding Cultural Diversity in Business.* London, UK and Boston, MA: Nicholas Brealey, 2006.

Tylor, E.B. *Primitive Culture.* London, UK: Cambridge Books, 1913.

Walker, D.; T. Walker; and J. Schmitz. *Doing Business Internationally.* New York, NY: McGraw-Hill, 2003.

Ury, W. *The Power of a Positive NO: How to Say NO & Still Get to YES.* London, UK: Hodder & Stoughton, 2008.

Ury, W. *Getting Past NO.* New York, NY: Bantam Books, 2007.

Index

OTHER TITLES IN THE INTERNATIONAL BUSINESS COLLECTION

Tamer Cavusgil, Georgia State, Michael Czinkota, Georgetown, and Gary Knight, Florida State University, Editors

- *Trade Promotion Strategies: Best Practices* by Claude Cellich and Michel Borgeon
- *As I Was Saying...: Observations on International Business and Trade Policy, Exports, Education, and the Future* by Michael Czinkota
- *China: Doing Business in the Middle Kingdom* by Stuart Strother
- *Essential Concepts of Cross-Cultural Management: Building on What We All Share* by Lawrence A. Beer
- *As the World Turns...: Observations on International Business and Policy, Going International and Transition* by Michael Czinkota
- *Assessing and Mitigating Business Risks in India* by Balbir Bhasin
- *The Emerging Markets of the Middle East: Strategies for Entry and Growth* by Tim Rogmans
- *Doing Business in China: Getting Ready for the Asian Century* by Jane Menzies, Mona Chung, and Stuart Orr
- *Transfer Pricing in International Business: A Management Tool for Adding Value* by Geoff Turner
- *Management in Islamic Countries: Principles and Practice* by UmmeSalma Mujtaba Husein
- *Burma: Business and Investment Opportunities in Emerging Myanmar* by Balbir Bhasin
- *Global Business and Corporate Governance: Environment, Structure, and Challenges* by John Thanopoulos

Announcing the Business Expert Press Digital Library

*Concise E-books Business Students Need
for Classroom and Research*

This book can also be purchased in an e-book collection by your library as
- a one-time purchase,
- that is owned forever,
- allows for simultaneous readers,
- has no restrictions on printing, and
- can be downloaded as PDFs from within the library community.

Our digital library collections are a great solution to beat the rising cost of textbooks. E-books can be loaded into their course management systems or onto student's e-book readers.

The **Business Expert Press** digital libraries are very affordable, with no obligation to buy in future years. For more information, please visit **www.businessexpertpress.com/librarians**. To set up a trial in the United States, please email **sales@businessexpertpress.com**.

www.ingramcontent.com/pod-product-compliance
Lightning Source LLC
Chambersburg PA
CBHW051520170526
45165CB00002B/537

*9 7 8 1 6 0 6 4 9 8 0 6 4 *